14.95

The Last Picture Show: *Bookmarked*

Larry McMurtry's
The Last Picture Show:

BOOKMARKED

STEVE YARBROUGH

Kirby Gann, *Series Editor*

PUBLISHING

Ig Publishing
Box 2547
New York, NY 10163
www.igpub.com

ISBN: 978-1-63246-049-3

PRINTED IN THE UNITED STATES OF AMERICA

FIRST EDITION | FIRST PRINTING

WHAT MAKES US SUSCEPTIBLE TO THE CHARMS OF CERTAIN books?

This is a question I've pondered a lot lately. It seems to me that more and more, readers want to read novels about people who, as I've heard it put numerous times, "are just like me." If they're from the South, they like books set in the South. If they're from Boston, they like books set in New England or at least someplace no farther away than New York. If they grew up in a migrant household in California's San Joaquin Valley, they can't relate to the work of writers like John Cheever or John Updike: those guys are part of the dominant culture and their characters never seem to lack money, so what's the problem? Add to these tendencies the preference for particular narrative approaches—"I only enjoy speculative fiction," etc.—and you're left with a lot of people whose reading interests are very narrow. The notion that great literature, like great music, is a product of cross-fertilization has come under siege.

The writer I think of as my mentor, the late novelist William Harrison, who taught in the University of Arkansas's MFA program and exerted a strong influence on writers as different as Barry Hannah, Lee K. Abbott, Ellen Gilchrist and John Dufresne, had a well-defined aesthetic. The most succinct way to describe it would be to say that he was a traditional realist with a pronounced preference for the masculine. The writers he admired and held up as models were Chekhov, Conrad, Hemingway, Fitzgerald, Graham Greene and Richard Yates. Yet some of his own novels and stories, particularly a handful of shorter pieces like "Down the Blue Hole," published by Gordon Lish in *Esquire*, and "Rollerball Murder," which provided the basis for the film *Rollerball*, are written in a very different vein. Either of them could conceivably pass as a Donald Barthelme story.

Born in Fort Worth, not far from where *The Last Picture Show* is set, Bill was hostile to Southern fiction and, if he were still around to read this, would surely object to my use of a capital letter in the word "Southern." He considered most of Faulkner's work overwrought and convoluted and was particularly dismissive of *Absalom, Absalom!* "It may be your favorite novel," he once told me, "but as far as I'm concerned, Thomas Sutpen is nothing but a vague Southern presence." He was not fond of Eudora Welty, though he had some tolerance for Robert Penn Warren and *All the King's Men*, and he expressed grudging admiration for Flannery O'Connor, while correctly noting that she was probably the writer most likely to spell doom for me, since I admired her stories so much and was always trying to imitate her. "You use tougher language than she did," he said over the expensive dinner he'd bought me so I would be well-fed when he delivered bad news, "but your characters are mushy as hell, whereas hers are etched in stone." He said I shouldn't read another word by a Southerner until I turned forty.

The truth was that until I enrolled at Ole Miss as an undergraduate and fell under the spell of Faulkner and O'Connor, and a little later, Barry Hannah, I had never read Southern writers. Generally speaking, the last thing in the world I wanted to read was a novel that reminded me of my own life. By the time I reached high school, I was heavily into suspense fiction, particularly if it involved World War II. I loved reading books set in France and Germany and Poland, and I would have told you that my two favorite writers were Frederick Forsythe and Jack Higgins. I was also fond of Leon Uris and had read most of his novels, as well as a number of political thrillers like *Advise and Consent*, *Fail Safe* and *Seven Days in May*. I craved excitement and didn't see it in the day to day.

We label books that provide the kind of excitement I was looking for "escapist fare." Everyone understands that to mean that when we read them, we leave behind the cares of the world—the bills we can't pay, the bosses who dog our steps, the spouses we've fallen out of love with, if we ever loved them to begin with. I was too young to have any of those problems. What I wanted to escape from was a place.

Specifically, the house I had lived in since I was six years old and the father who, once his own dreams were extinguished, ruled it like Enver Hoxha presiding over Albania.

In a more general sense, I wanted to get as far away as I could from the Mississippi Delta. I was convinced that if I ever left, I would never go back. I have, of course, though only sporadically. Yet I wrote about it, and virtually no place else, for nearly forty years. The things that made it such a great place to write about also made it, for me at least, a terrible place to live.

The great alluvial floodplain is seventy miles across at its widest point. It extends from just south of Memphis to just north of Vicksburg. The landscape is as flat as the desktop I'm writing on, and once you leave town—there are no cities—the uniformity is undisturbed by any geographical features except the occasional creek or bayou, one of its three major rivers or the occasional clump of trees that probably never got cut down because the land was too swampy to farm. While the topsoil is still some of the most fertile on the planet, ten Delta counties are among the one hundred poorest in the country. Four are in the bottom twenty-five. One of those, Holmes, is next to last.

In the Delta of my youth—and, to a lesser extent, the Delta of today—your position is determined by how much land you own. True, there are bankers, lawyers, accountants and doctors and, by virtue of having college degrees and wearing dress shirts to work, they're accorded their share of prestige. But the bankers and the accountants and the most successful lawyers reap the greatest rewards from managing the financial affairs of the landowners. There is virtually no manufacturing sector in the Delta. There never has been. It's an agrarian culture, and while cotton is no longer king there, having first given way to catfish farming and more recently to corn, land remains the gold standard. In my high school locker room, before and after football practice, the most popular subject was sex. A close second was acreage. "How many acres does your daddy own?" I was glad that by the time I entered tenth grade, my father had given up farming, sparing me the need to face that question.

The late novelist Lewis "Buddy" Nordan, who grew up in nearby Itta Bena, once told me that as strange as it might seem to an outsider driving through the Delta for the first time, the vast flatness of the landscape made him claustrophobic. "Yes, you could see forever," he said, "but as far as you could see, you were seeing the same thing. No cities, not much color, just lots and lots of dirt." Perhaps it's not surprising that at the age of fifteen, Nordan bought a bus ticket and ran away to New York City, though it didn't take his mother and stepfather long to locate him and haul him back to Itta Bena.

Less enterprising than Nordan, I never set foot outside the South until 1983, by which time I was twenty-six years old. I traveled up the east coast with a friend from Arkansas, who had just sold his first novel to Simon & Schuster. We stopped in DC, Baltimore, and Philadelphia, taking in a baseball game in each city and visiting art museums. The accents were changing, but DC was full of Southerners, and so was Baltimore, and I felt pretty much at home in both of them. Philadelphia felt a little different, but I decided that was mostly because of the woman who sat behind us at Veterans' Stadium. Pete Rose was having a bad year with the Phillies, and he'd essentially been benched. When he came up to pinch hit in the bottom of the tenth, with a man on second and two outs, she formed a bullhorn with her hands and yelled, *"Pete, you're a fuckin' bum!"* Rose proceeded to line the first pitch off the wall in right-center, driving home the winning run. *"Atta fuckin' boy, Pete!"* the woman shrieked, leaping to her feet and spilling beer all over me.

The next day we took Amtrak into Manhattan. At Penn Station, we switched to the subway, finally emerging onto the sidewalk in Times Square, where all our senses came under assault. As soon as my friend had left me to go meet his editor, I went back downstairs, where I locked myself in a bathroom stall and hid money in my shoes. I was terrified. I remember thinking *These people are not like me. They are from a different planet.*

•

Despite my sometimes exasperated efforts to convince my students that they don't always profit from reading about people "just like" themselves, the book that spoke most resonantly to me when I was young—and continues to, I should add, even today—was about a character with whom I could easily identify. His name was Sonny Crawford, and he lived in a shabby little town, and he played football, and a war was going on, and he got along so badly with his drug-addicted father that he moved into a boarding house to live with his best friend. Also, he lusted after older women, and he got involved with one. But that didn't happen to him until about halfway through the book, and it didn't happen to me until a year or so after I'd read it.

I had heard about the film titled *The Last Picture Show*, of course, because when it came out in 1971, it was widely praised and frequently condemned. It wasn't shown in my hometown: in the late sixties, the Honey Theater had closed down, and even if it had still been open, that particular movie would not have been screened there. I knew nothing about it, except that it was supposedly outrageous and immoral. I didn't even know it was based on a novel.

So when a friend asked me if I wanted to borrow his copy of a book with that title, I asked him what it was about.

"Among other things," he said, "it's about football and sex."

Either of those topics would have brought an affirmative reply. The two of them together promised pure bliss. And anyway, I trusted my friend's taste. The previous year he had loaned me the *Sports Illustrated* writer Dan Jenkins' novel *Semi-Tough*, about a Texan named Billy Clyde Puckett who plays for the New York Giants, and I had already read it twice. In that particular book, the characters are as broad as Texas itself, and most if not all of the humor is scatological:

jokes about farting consume page upon page. I assumed *The Last Picture Show* was written in the same vein.

I did not understand, and would not have cared to understand, the difference between art and truth. But suffice it to say that if someone had told me *The Last Picture Show* was literature, I would not have gone anywhere near it. Literature, to me, meant books like *Silas Marner*, which I was supposed to read but hadn't. At the time, I was at best a C student, and I had even failed a class or two. Since the toughest football practices of the week were usually on Tuesdays, I typically gave myself those mornings off from school, showing up for fifth and six periods, then going over to the locker room to get dressed. My father was working eighteen-hour shifts and, on his days off, he slept of necessity until afternoon himself. My mom was working at a store in town, and she left early for work and had given up trying to make me do anything I didn't want to. I was enjoying a little freedom for the first time in my life. Since I was the best player on a very good team, my quirks were tolerated. At that school, nothing mattered more than football, and most of my teachers probably figured I'd never be good at anything else anyway, since I'd never given them any reason to think otherwise. Once I'd made my final tackle, I could safely be reconsigned to the poor-white ranks. Former classmates, should they encounter me on Front Street, would nod at me like their parents nodded at my father. The rest of the time, I'd remain forgotten.

THE FRIEND WHO LOANED ME THAT COPY OF *THE LAST Picture Show* was called Rev. A recent transplant from Arkansas and the son of the Episcopal minister, he played strong safety, and his real name is Bill Lancaster. Everybody on the football team at my small, all-white Delta school in the early seventies had a nickname. The tallest of my teammates, a lineman who went on to play for Mississippi State, was known as Lurch, after the six-foot-nine-inch butler on *The Adams Family*. Our skinny quarterback was called Stick, and our fullback, whose last name was Arant, was called Ahab. I played guard on offense and tackle on defense. My nickname was Yarddog.

Nicknames, we understood, were supposed to capture something essential in the character or appearance of the individual on whom they were conferred. In recent years quite a few of the guys I played with have become my Facebook friends, and judging from their occasional posts about my athletic exploits, I am lodged in their memories as a particularly vicious competitor, though that is not how I remember my younger self. One of them maintains that I was given my nickname because of the popular Jim Croce tune "Bad, Bad Leroy Brown" (*the baddest man in the whole damn town/meaner than old King Kong/meaner than a junkyard dog*). But since the head coach started calling me that at the beginning of my sophomore year, when I was still only a backup and frequently got castigated for lack of "intestinal fortitude"—the worst thing you could say about a football player—I think I was tagged with it for at least two different reasons. The first, and most obvious, was that it began with the same three letters as my last name. The second, and to my mind more revealing, was that like a yarddog, I was perceived as an outlier.

"You looked different from everybody else," Rev said a couple years ago when he came to dinner at our home in Massachusetts. A successful attorney, he lives in Mobile and was in Boston on legal business. "You dressed differently, you talked differently, and you must have thought differently, too, else you probably wouldn't have turned into a writer. Because let's face it, Yarddog, most folks never have *read* a book, let alone written one."

I'd seen Rev only a couple of times in nearly forty years. The first of those encounters happened back in 1990, when he came to a book signing in Jackson to purchase a copy of my story collection *Family Men*. It was the first book I'd ever published, and I saw a number of friends from high school that day, as well as a few of their parents, a couple of former teachers and our old principal. Rev was the one I spent the most time talking to. For one thing, I'd been closer to him than anyone else who showed up, and for another, he was a lawyer. Though I hadn't been nervous about the stories when I wrote them, or when they appeared, as most of them had, in literary magazines, I had suddenly gotten plenty nervous at the thought that quite a few people from my hometown were about to read my work. Unlike Larry McMurtry, who turned Archer City, Texas, into the town of Thalia in *The Last Picture Show*, I called my hometown by its real name in my stories, and nearly all of them were set there.

He told me he'd talked to a couple of people who'd already read the book, though it had only been out for ten days or so, and I suspect a tremor crept into my voice when I wondered aloud if any of them were mad.

"Why would anybody be mad?" he asked.

By then we were alone at the table where I'd been signing, and though it amuses me now, after many years worth of book events where attendance has fluctuated between perhaps a hundred people on an exceptionally good night and zero on an exceptionally bad night and twenty-five or thirty on most nights, I was relieved that nobody else wanted to buy my collection. It was a strange feeling and one that I have experienced, to varying degrees, at readings and signings for each of my nine books.

"Maybe they'll think they see themselves or something."

"Assuming they did," Rev said, "it seems to me there

are two possible outcomes. The first is that they'll be proud they saw themselves, in which case you won't have anything to worry about. The other is that they'll be ashamed of seeing themselves, in which case you probably won't have anything to worry about either, because they're not going to want anybody to think you were writing about *them*."

In the main, what he predicted that day has proven true, though exceptions have occurred. About sixteen or seventeen years ago, after my novel *The Oxygen Man* appeared, it got back to me that the father of a former high school teammate said if he ever heard I was visiting my hometown, he'd start chewing tobacco, in hopes he'd get a chance to cover me with brown spit. I also learned that the father of another friend went around announcing that all of my works should be permanently banned in Sunflower County. And my father informed me that a man he used to work for, one of the two or three wealthiest in town, had stopped him in Wal-Mart and told him I needed to clean up my language. By this time, I was hardened, so I asked what tone his ex-boss had used.

"Why?"

"Because if he said it the wrong way, I'm going to call him up and tell him to fuck himself."

"Oh, he said it in a real nice tone," my father assured me.

As Rev noted over dinner, most people are not readers, and nobody else that I grew up with became a writer. And I felt sure that back in the early seventies, if you'd asked any of our teachers which of us might turn into one, none of them would have named me. I'd no sooner entertained that thought than Rev said, "If you had to pick one person you knew when you were young who did the most to help you become a novelist, who would it be?"

Over the rim of my glass, I studied my old friend. Whereas I still weigh about what I did when I played football—235, give or take a pound—he's gotten a little heavier. Back then, he was undersized, 160, I'm going to guess, a safety who covered much larger tight ends and often had to come up from the secondary and take on pulling guards my size or even bigger. While most people faced with that task might have tried to go around blockers or just get out of their way, Rev met them head on, often smashing a forearm into their facemasks or taking their legs out from under them. He played like a demon. Sometimes he stopped when the whistle blew. Sometimes he didn't.

I refilled his glass, then told him that *he* had done the most to help me become a novelist. He got a good laugh out of that, thinking it was a joke. Should he happen to read this, I hope he will soon understand that it was not.

If, as Rev had remarked, I dressed differently from the majority of my classmates, it was because most of their families had a lot more money than mine did. The school was one of the private "segregation academies" that sprang up all over Mississippi in the years after *Brown v. Board of Education*, and the tuition consumed a significant portion of my parents' income. Though I didn't know it at the time, they borrowed so much money to keep me at the Academy that they wouldn't pay off the debt until I was nearly thirty. But cheaper and less fashionable clothing was not the only reason I looked different. In an era of shaggy males, my father, who sported the same crew cut he'd worn in the Navy, insisted my hair be kept short, my ears and collar fully exposed. Short hair consigned one to the status of a redneck. Add to that the fact that neither of my parents had a college degree, that they hadn't even finished high school, and maybe you can begin to appreciate what I was up against.

Until spinal problems turned him into a man who stooped over and walked with a cane, my father stood six-foot-four. In 1944, his height had helped him convince a Navy recruiter that he must be at least eighteen years old, which he was not, and he quit school and joined up. Though the IQ test he was administered yielded a score of 138, he didn't make the cut to enter radar training and instead spent most of his service in the engine room of the *USS Atlanta*. After the war, he came home and tried to make it as a farmer—a lost cause if, like him, you didn't own a sliver of land. In the years before my birth, he also worked as a mechanic and drove a "rolling store" that traveled the countryside selling items like neckbones, soft drinks, candy, ice cream and tobacco to field hands and their children. By the time I was born, in 1956, he was back in the agricultural sector, partnering with my maternal grandfather, farming a few hundred acres of land they rented from the county. Between then and when I graduated from high school, he gave up farming to work for a local petroleum company, gave that up to run two different cotton gins, went back to farming and, in the evenings, studied electronics through a correspondence course. Around 1970, he earned an FCC broadcast license and shortly thereafter went to work running a transmitter for Mississippi Educational Television Network, the job he kept until retirement.

My mother didn't work until I entered middle school. I suspect that my father disallowed it, probably because he would have considered it a sign of his own improvidence to have a working wife. If that was not the reason, I can't fathom what the reason was, since he rarely let more than a couple of days pass without reminding me how "purr" we were. He disallowed her a lot of things. For instance, she was not allowed to write a check, and after he quarreled with our minister, who had told the congregation that if we were really Christians we would welcome black people to our worship services, she was not allowed to attend church. When she did go to work, it was as a checkout clerk at United Dollar Store. My guess is that a few years worth of paying tuition at the all-white private school forced him to swallow his pride.

For most of my childhood, we lived about six miles north of town, in a house that he somehow managed to buy in 1962. A dingy, boxy three-bedroom with sheetrock siding, it had been built a couple of feet off the ground, to allow water to pass beneath it in the event of a flood. A large drainage ditch named Beaverdam Creek lay only fifty yards away, and in the spring, when the Mississippi backed up into local tributaries like the Sunflower, the Tallahatchie and the Yazoo, those rivers overflowed into the Delta's creeks and bayous. Once or twice a year, for all seventeen years that my parents owned the house, there were floods. The water never entered the house itself, but we were often cut off for days at a time, able to leave only on tractors or, once, in a rowboat. What did enter the house in several instances was water moccasins. We never saw them when they were in there, but we found their shed skins in drawers and closets. This seemed normal enough to me at the time.

The other thing that didn't trouble me overly much was that I slept in a bedroom where the son of the previous owners had killed his brother with a gun he thought was unloaded. Such occurrences were not that infrequent then (nor are they today) because virtually everybody in the Delta is armed and guns have a way of going off. Also, I had until then lived in a trailer parked in my maternal grandparents' back yard. At least for the first few years we lived in an honest-to-God house, it seemed luxurious. Our yard was capacious, with a couple of towering pecan trees and three decrepit outbuildings—a garage, a smokehouse and a barn—that initially seemed to offer all sorts of possibilities for play.

The problem was that once I went to the Academy, in fourth grade, there was seldom anyone to play with. The only kids who lived close by were black, and I had learned the hard way that playing with them would get me whipped with my father's leather belt if he found out. Their parents didn't want them playing with me, either, knowing all too well what kind of trouble crossing the color line could bring to their doorstep. A few classmates came to my house once, but hardly anyone ever came twice and after a while my father refused to let me invite them. When I asked why, he simply said, "I don't want your feelings hurt."

Children are masters of untempered cruelty, and my feelings had already been hurt. One classmate gleefully told me that when his mother drove up in front of our house, she said, "That place looks like where the Beverly Hillbillies lived before they took off for California." Another asked me simply, "How come you got such a lousy house?"

Though their homes don't look grand to me today, they did at the time. Some of them had a second story, and a few even had swimming pools out back. I occasionally got invited to sleepovers—usually, I expect, because no one else was available—but by sixth or seventh grade the invitations had dried up. Middle school seems to be a miserable time for lots of people, and I was among their number. I will admit, though, that from the distance of nearly fifty years I sometimes view those days through the golden mist of nostalgia. True, the country was coming apart at the seams, and we were mired down in Vietnam, which I vaguely understood might eventually pose a threat to my existence. But having few options other than to find happiness in something besides friendship, I was learning just how much joy books could provide.

My reading, when I think back on it, seems an unlikely blend of adult and adolescent fare. A Hardy Boys mystery might be followed by a volume of popular history by Bruce Catton, Shelby Foote, or Cornelius Ryan. Every few months I reread *The Adventures of Huckleberry Finn*. I read copies of *True Confessions* that I found hidden beneath the lingerie in my mother's dresser, and I read Tex Maule's boys' books about a fictitious LA Rams team and Wilfred McCormick's Bronc Burnett novels and Erle Stanley Gardner's Perry

Mason novels. Every now and then, usually by accident, I came across something a little more elevated. At twelve or thirteen, I discovered a couple of John O'Hara titles left behind by my recently deceased great-grandmother, and I devoured *Pal Joey* and *Appointment in Samarra*. When I went to the local library hoping to find more of O'Hara's work, the librarian, who was known Miss LuAnn, said she would need written permission from one of my parents before I could withdraw "things of that nature." A few days later, I returned to present her with a note, allegedly composed by my mother. *Please allow my son Stevie Yarbrough to check out any and all books by the classic author John O'Hara.* Miss LuAnn smiled, slipped it in her desk, then said, "Okay, Stevie, go get them. If your momma complains, I'll remind her she wrote me this note." I went home with *Ten North Frederick* and *Elizabeth Appleton*, cautiously concealing them between a pair of Nancy Drew mysteries.

A NOVELIST I KNOW—A MAN ABOUT MY AGE, WHOSE parents were both New York literary figures, well-published if not well-paid—once said that while it made perfect sense for him to have become a writer, it made no sense at all for me to. How, he wondered, did something so strange and unlikely come to pass?

When he posed this question, we were relaxing in the Jacuzzi in my back yard in California, having a final drink after a party my wife and I had thrown in his honor. It might reflect a kinder light upon me if I could tell you that I did not find the question offensive, but that would be giving myself far too much credit. In truth, my head filled up with red fog, as it tends to when the polite persona I have spent most of my life cultivating melts like the Wicked Witch of the West. I don't know for sure what I said to him, but since we have remained on speaking terms, I feel certain I did not tell him to go to hell.

Instead, I imagine I relayed an anecdote that I like to trot out when people ask me a version of the question he asked that night. I suspect I prefaced the anecdote, as I almost always do, with the observation that though my father had very little education, he was always an avid reader and that he helped instill in me a love of books. I may have told him how much my dad enjoyed Larry McMurtry's work, especially *Lonesome Dove* and its prequels and sequels, along with their less literary antecedents like the novels of Zane Grey and Louis L'Amour. After that, I most likely went on to relate how one night, I walked into my parents' bedroom to find my dad sprawled across the mattress, still wearing his work pants that were streaked with dust from the cotton fields (if I presented him as a farmer) or covered in lint (if I presented him as the operator of a cotton gin). He had a big leather-bound book, I probably told my friend, and when I asked what he was reading, my father said, "Son, it's a long poem called *Paradise Lost*. A fellow named John Milton wrote it. It's some of the most beautiful language I ever read."

It's reasonable to think the other writer in my Jacuzzi shook his head in wonder, that perhaps he was deeply moved, as people often are by that anecdote. But since he's a novelist himself and well-versed in the art of fabrication, it's also reasonable to think he doubted whether the anecdote contained even a shred of literal truth.

It did. I do recall my father reading *Paradise Lost*, but I don't know exactly when it happened, and I don't know if he was lying across the bed when I saw him with the book, or if he was sitting on the couch or the front porch. What I am certain of, though, is that it happened before he had the argument with our preacher about race. I know what made him read John Milton: he had decided to become a poet—specifically, a religious poet—and he had also decided to become an evangelist. A man I knew as Brother Joe provided the impetus.

Brother Joe was the predecessor of Brother William, the minister with whom my father quarreled. Brother William was old, probably in his mid-seventies, whereas Brother Joe was young and vigorous, nearly as tall as my father, if memory serves, and a good bit more muscular. I remember the day he came to preach a trial sermon as part of his job interview. He delivered his homily, then retired with his family to a small office behind the baptistery while the congregation, led by the board of deacons, of which my father was not yet a member but soon would be, debated his suitability. At the end of the discussion, he was accepted by acclamation. I had liked his sermon, insofar as I could like anything that prevented me from seeing the first quarter of a football game, but I had no say-so because I was only about seven or eight at the time and not yet saved. My deliverance from evil would come a few years later, when Brother William submerged me beneath the cleansing waters.

Brother Joe spent a lot of time on my father. His first task was to officially convert him, since my dad was a life-long Methodist who attended the Baptist church because my mother went there but also because the only Methodist church was in town and its membership overlapped with the country club set. The conversion didn't take long. I recall seeing him baptized in the same glass-fronted tank where I would soon undergo immersion.

Brother Joe continued to pay us frequent visits, and each time he came he brought at least two books. The first, inevitably, was the Bible. The second would be something secular. He introduced my dad to the work of Bruce Catton and Shelby Foote—not just Foote's Civil War histories, either, but his novels as well—and up until a few years ago, when he suffered a series of strokes and lost much of his eyesight, my father regularly reread Foote's Delta novel *Love in a Dry Season* and seldom passed up the chance to tell me that I, too, might have written a book that good if I hadn't married a foreigner and spent so much time in places where I didn't belong.

Brother Joe had a divinity degree from the Baptist Seminary in New Orleans, and though I have no idea how he would strike me if I had met him as an adult, when I was a child he seemed brilliant. Unlike the fiery Brother Blanton, the minister in *The Last Picture Show*, he did not rail day and night about sin and damnation. He never raised his voice. He quoted from sources other than the Bible, including Shakespeare's sonnets, and he must have been the one who clued my father into Milton.

My dad began to write poems, an entire book of them. He called it *The Kingdom Childe*. The poems were handwritten in a yellow spiral notebook, with no cross-outs or other signs of revision. He may have written and revised them on loose sheets and then copied the finished versions into the notebook, but I don't recall finding any discarded pages around the house or in the trash, and my suspicion is that he just wrote them as they came to him and that was that. Most of the poems were about Jesus, but quite a few were about me and at least one was about my mother. He sometimes came into my room and read them to me at bedtime. All of them rhymed, and though it would be a long time before I learned about the ballad stanza, I think most if not all of them were written in that form. They were also composed in some approximation of King James English. The poem I remember best was one in which my father wrote about how he "stole" into my room one night and knelt by my bed to give thanks for my existence. More than half a century later, I recall the last lines, which seemed to be addressed to the almighty. "I brush a tear from mine own eye/as Thou didst brush from Thine."

I heard him tell my mother that he had shown the book to Brother Joe and that Brother Joe said, "This *is* poetry, John." My father took the minister's response as evidence that his work was both accomplished and profound, and one night when he came to read to me, he told me that the next day he would send the manuscript off to a publisher, so that other fathers could buy it and read it to their own sons.

That was the last I ever heard of *The Kingdom Childe*.

•

His desire to become an evangelist was also kindled by Brother Joe.

Though I can remember the minister's face, I can't recall anything about his wife or his children, not even how many kids he had. I don't remember where he came from, but I know he was not local, and what sticks in my mind is that he grew up somewhere in east Mississippi. It seems likely to me that he also grew up poor, because my father was completely at home around him, whereas he was never comfortable around people who either came from money or had managed to acquire it. In Brother Joe, I suspect, my father saw an idealized version of himself. Brother Joe served a higher power and kept his hands clean, whereas my father lived a life of dirt and grime and counted himself lucky if he managed to make the payments on our house and keep my mother and me fed. His intelligence had not served him, or anyone else, well. Other men would nod if they encountered him on Front Street on Saturday afternoons, when almost everybody went to town, but he slipped right out of their thoughts the moment they passed him by. He might as well have been invisible.

All of this changed when Brother Joe began to pay him special attention. After he was baptized, the minister asked him to serve as an usher, so every Sunday, both morning and evening, my father would move along one of the aisles, collecting the offering plate at the end of each row and handing it to the first person in the next row. When those plates, which were made of dark hardwood and had red felt-lined bottoms, reached the back of the church, they were always full of money, and though it did not occur to me at the time, the sight of all that green paper must have been hard for him to bear. I know it was rough on me. I had seen plenty of fives, tens, twenties and fifties in those plates, and on one memorable occasion I even spotted a hundred-dollar bill, which was probably more than my father earned in a week.

By the time he began to talk about becoming an evangelist, he was running the first of the two cotton gins that he would operate over the next few years. The co-owners of this particular gin were, like my father, deacons at the church, and both of them owned a lot of rich Delta farmland and were cotton farmers themselves. One of them, Brother George, was also the choir director.

He had a nickname: Tiny. I'm not sure anybody except my father ever called him that, though, and I strongly doubt he ever called him that to his face. Brother George, to say it simply, was anything but small. While not exactly fat, he was a man without angle; everything about him was soft and curved, even his chin. His stomach was pronounced, but it did not lap over his belt like those of so many men in a corner of the country that craves red meat and starch. His direction of the choir involved choosing which hymns would be sung at each service and, at least two or three Sundays a month, singing a solo in his velvety baritone. If he could read music, I saw no evidence of it, and he did no directing except for occasionally moving a couple of fingers on his right hand in time with the piano, which was played by his wife. When my father spoke of becoming an evangelist, he envisioned forming a team with Brother George, who would serve as his musical counterpart.

These were Godly times in our household at Route 2, Box 79. We prayed on Sunday mornings before attending church, we prayed in late afternoon before returning for the evening service and we prayed before Wednesday night's prayer meeting. My mother's prayers always began with the same seven words: "Dear God, we pray for them that's. . . ." What followed was always one of three adjectives. One time it would be "sick," the next time "hungry," the time after that "worried," and then she would start over. I can recall only one instance in which she deviated, and it surprised both my father and me so badly that we opened our eyes, as if to see whether we had imagined what we thought we'd just heard. The look on his face assured me we had not. "Dear God," she had said, "I pray for them that's overbearin'. Please let them that's overbearin' feel somebody bearin' down on them like they bear down on others. Bring 'em low, Lord, so they'll know."

My own specialty was prayer for those who drank—chief among them such wayward kin as Uncle Henry, Uncle Billy, Uncle Cecil and Uncle Pat. About all you had to do to make my prayer list was to be spotted with a beer in your hand. I also prayed for the father of the only other white boy who lived nearby, a kid named Benny whose family was so uncouth that they continued to send their son to the public school where, it was alleged, he ate lunch at the same table as the black students. His father drove around in an old pickup, and my recollection is that he always looked unshaven. Rumor had it that he often tossed empty Schlitz cans into the road ditch.

As befit one who believed he'd gotten The Call, my father, who always prayed last, cast his net on stormy seas. At various times I heard him pray for George Wallace, whose presidential campaign he supported; for the health of "Ike," whom he continued to admire despite his having ordered troops into Little Rock; for the demise of rock music and a return to manly hairstyles; for a new prohibition act; for a new Supreme Court; for rain; for clear skies; for black people to regain their senses and accept their place like they used to; for Russia to become a Christian nation; for the local poolhall to close down; for the Honey Theater to quit showing unwholesome movies and, should they refuse, for the Lord to shut it down too. He prayed for my mother and me: that I would never drink or take drugs and that when I reached my majority I would find a good job in town at a store like the Western Auto, so I would not have to toil in the fields as he had; that my mother would remain a dedicated homemaker "as Thy will demands" and that her hands would not become chapped and broken from washing dishes and shelling snap beans and black-eyed peas.

Amen.

As I write, my father is lying in a hospital in Greenville, Mississippi, some twenty-five miles from the town where he lived for eighty-nine years, save for when he served in the

Navy and traveled to various parts of the country, as well as the South Pacific and Japan. The strokes have robbed him of the ability to speak clearly, to walk or use his hands. A few weeks ago he fell out of his wheelchair at a rehab facility and broke several vertebra. He had to be placed in a neck cast, and within a couple of weeks he became nonresponsive. Right now, he is being given glucose, but since he long ago signed a Do Not Resuscitate form that prevents the use of a feeding tube, he is essentially waiting to die. According to what the hospital has told me, his life expectancy at this point is less than a month.

Thinking back over the portion of his life that I've witnessed, I feel fairly certain that for him the happiest period was those days in the mid-to-late sixties when he wrote poetry and dreamed of preaching the gospel. I think it was probably the only time when he felt he was moving in a clear direction, that he was doing something other than staggering from one day to the next, trying not to drown in despair. Nobody, except perhaps Brother Joe, would have given him a dime's chance of attaining his goal, and even my father himself must have secretly feared it would never come to fruition, since nothing else ever had. But if he entertained such doubts, he never showed it. He smiled a lot in those days, though he has seldom smiled since. It was as if he'd been administered a wonder drug that briefly overcame his dark disposition. I don't recall being whipped much, if at all, and a couple of times I saw him embrace my mother, something I had not seen before and would never see again.

•

The life of a gin operator is a seasonal affair. For the first six months of the year, you have almost no responsibilities. Preparation starts in early summer, when you have to check all the machinery, making sure the belts are in good condition, that all the nuts and bolts are tight, the saws properly lubricated. From the day you gin the first bale, around the end of August or beginning of September, until you gin the last one, usually before Thanksgiving, you don't have time to do much of anything else. My father came home after midnight and left the following morning while I was still asleep. When I got to the breakfast table, his Scofield Reference Bible, which he prized for its concordance, was invariably lying beside his empty coffee cup, the black ribbon that served as a marker visible between the gilded pages. He studied it every morning and again when he got home.

After he sent his poems off to be rejected, he began to write sermons. Some of these he worked on in the gin office that looked out onto the scales, where cotton trailers were weighed before the man operating the suction pipe went to work. But most of the homilies were written in his bedroom during the winter and spring. They ran to ten or twelve pages apiece. He composed them on yellow legal pads and generally kept them locked away in the closet along with his rifles and shotguns, but once or twice I saw a pad lying on the desk that doubled as his chest of drawers.

I don't remember much about the sermons, how the writing struck me, but I can say that though he had never written an academic paper in his life, he knew something about citations: the pages were often footnoted, and the footnotes contained abbreviations that I did not understand, like *Cf.* and *N.B.*

One Sunday morning, for the only time in his life, he stood behind a pulpit to preach.

I suspect this happened in 1966, though I could be off a year in either direction. I know it was in late spring or early summer, because he wore the lighter of his two suits, and I recall it as a beautiful day, not yet hot, with the odor of cape jasmine in the air. Brother Joe was off preaching a week-long revival similar to the one that figures prominently in *The Last Picture Show*, and he had asked my father to deliver the morning sermon. The practice was not uncommon. In cases in which, for whatever reason, the minister was absent, deacons were often asked to fill in. It happened three or four times a year.

By tradition, the family of the preacher sat in the front row. But my father did not want my mother and me to sit there, telling us to take our places in a pew at the rear of the sanctuary. "When pride cometh," he said, quoting from *Proverbs*, "then cometh shame; but with the lowly is wisdom."

We were the lowly, my mother and I, a fact that by then both of us accepted. Anyway, I was happy to escape scrutiny. I figured he'd make a fool of himself. Judging from the expressions on the faces of some of the choir members when he laid his Bible on the pulpit, I was not alone.

I wish I could hear his sermon again. As it was, I got to hear it twice: it was taped and broadcast on the local radio station the following week. If this seems odd, it's important to know that many of the churches recorded Sunday morning services for broadcast, and that each weekday morning you could hear somebody preaching on WNLA.

It's tempting to try to write the kind of sermon my father might have delivered, then present it to the reader as fact. But the truth is that I don't have the faintest notion what he said that day, though I heard one of my Uncle Lamar's daughters, who had been raised Catholic, tell him, "Uncle Johnny, you were preaching fire and brimstone. You sounded real good on the radio, though."

I don't remember any fire or brimstone. What I remember is how he looked and how I felt while he was up there. The pulpit stood on a platform that was two or three feet higher than the main floor, and when you added my father's height to it, you were confronted by an imposing figure. I had been scared of him all my life and would remain so until I started lifting weights and became much bulkier and stronger than he had ever been. But that day, for at least an hour, he ceased to frighten me. He stood there in his beige suit, which had been bought at a secondhand store in Greenwood, and addressed the congregation in calm, measured tones. He didn't pound the lectern or gesture wildly or turn red in the face like so many preachers I'd seen. He exuded both confidence and humility and—dare I say it—grace. For the first time in my life, I was proud of him.

He didn't manage to save anyone that day—least of all himself—but during the hymn of invitation, a couple of people came forward to rededicate their faith. Afterwards, my father stood with them before the altar and delivered the benediction. Then he made his way down the aisle and stood at the church door, like Brother Joe always did, shaking hands with members of the congregation as they filed out into the parking lot. Several people told my mother what a fine job he'd done, and I heard one of them say "He's a natural," though I wasn't exactly certain what that meant.

·

In the end, it meant nothing at all. No matter what my father attempted, he nearly always ended up facing a closed door.

One day Brother Joe drove over and informed my parents that he and his family would be moving away. "We're going to starve to death here," my mother told me he said. I'm not one hundred percent certain, but I believe he left the ministry entirely. What happened to him is one of many questions I would like to ask my father, but he can no longer answer. And even if he could, he might chose not to. There have always been subjects he would not discuss with me. Something tells me this might be one of them.

Brother Joe, as I said earlier, was replaced by Brother

William, a stolid man who spoke with a patrician accent and had formerly served as the pastor of a big church in Jackson. Though he'd been retired for several years, he told us he believed God wanted him to return to the pulpit and help shepherd us through challenging times. Immediately, he began to set a new tone.

Since the church's lack of funds was the reason for the prior minister's departure, he said, it was important to insist that all members perform their Christian duty, tithing a tenth of their income to the church each Sunday. Shortly thereafter, each family was issued a green and white box, and inside the box were fifty-two envelopes—one for each Sunday of the year—with the last name of the family pre-printed in the upper left-hand corner. Beneath the name was the phrase *Amount Tithed*, followed by a blank. From then on, Brother William announced, people should use the envelopes rather than just dropping bills into the collection plate. Children could continue to put coins in the plate, unless their weekly allowance was more than ten dollars, in which case their contributions should be placed in the envelope with their parents'.

Brother William also began to speak about politics. Along with Brother George and his partner in the gin company and a handful of others who owned their own farmland, Brother William was a member of the Republican Party, at that time a beleaguered minority in Mississippi and, as odd as this sounds now, the more progressive of the two parties at the state level when it came to the question of race. He urged that members of the congregation give serious thought before casting their ballots, and he stopped just short of proclaiming that if Jesus himself were allowed to vote, he would cast *His* ballot for Richard Nixon.

Each Sunday, when we drove away from church, my father was a little angrier than he'd been the week before. He didn't have to say anything for my mother and me to know how mad he was—both of us were human seismographs—but he said plenty, usually before we'd gotten out of the gravel lot.

"The nerve of that old blowhard," he seethed one morning, whacking the steering wheel, then starting the car. "Supposed to be preaching the word of God, and instead he's making campaign speeches."

My mother's method of dealing with his black fits was to change the subject to some innocuous topic and chatter away, in the vain hope that if she could only talk long enough, the storm would blow over. "Mildred Boone just told me they're fixin' to make a movie in Carrollton," she said, beginning her sad filibuster. "Claims it'll have Steve McQueen and Will Geer in it, and she didn't know who all else. Said it's based on some book by somebody or other—"

"It's based on a book by Faulkner," my dad said. "Not that it matters, and since it don't, just shut up about it. Most of them people back there stink. Letting that old man dictate to 'em like he was God hisself rather than just his servant. It makes me want to puke."

Not long after that, Brother George told him that since

rain was in the forecast and everybody needed as many empty trailers as they could get, so they could pick the last of their crops before the bad weather hit, he would have to gin cotton on Sunday. My father carried his dark suit to the gin, worked until ten-thirty that morning, put it on and met my mother and me at church. That was the day Brother William told the congregation that if we were true Christians, we would welcome black people into our house of worship. Almost everybody smiled and ignored him, but my father did not, telling him off in the parking lot. That was the last time my family went to church.

I CAN MAKE ONLY AN EDUCATED GUESS WHERE I WAS when I read the first pages of *The Last Picture Show*. But I am going to go ahead and make it and say that I was sitting on the living room couch. That couch was covered in green fabric, which by this time was frayed in places, so that you could see the yellow foam of the seat cushions and backrest. To my right there's a television set, an old black-and-white Zenith console. My folks won't have a color TV until I leave for college. To my left, there's an armchair that matches the couch, right down to the fraying fabric. Directly in front of me there's a spindly coffee table, on top of which stands a big ashtray that nobody has used since my father quit smoking nearly ten years ago. In the corner next to the window that opens onto the screened porch, there's an overstuffed rocker that has a big gash in the seat cushion, which my father has concealed beneath several strips of black electrician's tape.

A couple of months ago—for I'm thinking I read the

book in the summer before my senior year—a man named Jake Gibbs sat in that rocking chair. My father and mother and I all sat on the couch, and another man, whom I will call Mr. B, sat in the matching armchair. Jake Gibbs was once an All-American quarterback at Ole Miss and, following that, the starting catcher for the New York Yankees. When he came to visit us, he was the head baseball coach at Ole Miss and also a recruiter for the football team. Mr. B was a local farmer who owned a lot of land near the Sunflower River and had once played football at Ole Miss with Jake Gibbs. They came to discuss the possibility of my receiving an athletic scholarship to play for the Rebels. The main things I recall about the conversation are Mr. B shaking his head and musing about the high cost of college and Jake Gibbs talking about how the athletic cafeteria fed the members of the football team all they could eat. If you wanted three steaks for supper, he said, they were yours for the taking, free and clear. I recall thinking how great it was going to be when Ole Miss signed me, how I'd have it made and finally be able to leave this place I was starting to hate.

Unfortunately, like my father, I was capable of harboring dreams that bordered on delusion. The programs that were printed for our high school games added a couple of inches to my height and about fifteen pounds of weight. Gibbs would have been able to take one look at me and figure out that I was not nearly as big as the roster stated or as our game film might indicate. We only played against other all-white teams, and I was nearly always bigger and faster than the lackluster competition. Come national signing day, only one Division 1 school would make me an offer—the University of Southern Mississippi—and by then I would have panicked and signed with a tiny Division II school, where I would never play a down. A lot of my bubbles were about to burst.

Generally, no one sat in our living room except me, and I was most likely to sit there in the late afternoon, when I got back home from lifting weights. My mother never returned from the dollar store until after six, and my dad was often at the television station until well past midnight. On days when I knew he'd be at home, I remained at the gym until the coaches threw me out. I also spent a lot of time riding around on back roads, listening to the Allman Brothers, Marshall Tucker and the Charlie Daniels Band. Every now and then I had a date, but none of them led anywhere. The girls that really interested me all came from "better" families, and not even my ability on the football field could overcome that divide. It was a lonely time.

•

Sometimes Sonny felt like he was the only human creature in the town. It was a bad feeling, and it usually came on him in the mornings early, when the streets were completely empty, the way they were one Saturday morning in late November. The night before Sonny

had played his last game of football for Thalia
High School, but it wasn't that that made him
feel so strange and alone. It was just the look
of the town.

How that opening paragraph, composed when Larry
McMurtry was in his late twenties, would have struck me
at the age of seventeen is difficult to say. I wish I could
remember. My guess is that the first line touched a nerve,
because I had often felt like that myself. When I felt that
way, though, it was usually late at night. The third sentence,
I suspect, was a serious letdown. Rev had said the book was
about football. How the hell could it be about football if
the main character had already played his last game?

As is the case in nearly all of McMurtry's novels, the
opening chapter is heavy on exposition, as the author begins
to put the key pieces in play. In addition to meeting Sonny
Crawford, we are introduced to his best friend Duane; Sam
the Lion, "an old man . . . big and heavy, with a mane of
white hair," who seems to own about half of the businesses
in the town, including the poolhall, the café and the movie
theater; and a developmentally disabled boy named Billy,
who lives with Sam in a room above the poolhall and is
responsible for sweeping out all of the old man's properties. Sometimes, as in the opening pages, Billy sweeps right
out the door and down the street, often getting as far as the
city limit sign before someone picks him up, as Sonny does
on the morning the novel starts. We are also introduced

to Abilene, a driller for whom Duane works. Abilene has his own key to the poolhall and keeps an ivory-banded cue there in a padlocked rack. As the novel begins, he has come to collect on a bet he placed with Sam against the hometown team. They lost their final game badly, and Sonny was the goat, since two touchdowns were scored over his position on the defensive line. It's clear immediately that Sam and Abilene loathe each other, though it will be a while before we find out why.

The Last Picture Show, set during the early fifties when the Korean War is in progress, was McMurtry's third novel. The first, *Horseman, Pass By*, had earned widespread acclaim and been made into the successful film *Hud*, starring Paul Newman; the second, *Leaving Cheyenne*, received generally positive reviews. But the reception of *The Last Picture Show* was decidedly mixed. Kirkus found the book "chockablock with all the devices for teaching fictional heroes the facts of life one meets in print, with monotonous regularity," whereas *The New York Times* offered this bleak assessment: "Nothing much happens in Larry McMurtry's third novel. . . . But then nothing much happens in Thalia, the small Western town he is writing about. A sorrier place would be hard to find. It is desiccated and shabby physically, mean and small-minded spiritually. . . . It is a place in which a man can live all his life and end up feeling anonymous."

A book in which "nothing much happens" was not then, and is not now, a book for me. So I am lucky I never came across that review when it might have influenced me. There is something to be said for those pre-internet days, in which the opinions of strangers were not accessible with a couple taps of the iPhone. Back then, I read books either because I stumbled across them, read a few pages and liked them enough to continue, or because a person whose opinion I trusted told me they were good. If Rev liked it, I figured, there was a chance I would too. So I kept going, and while the next few chapters confirmed my fears that there would be no more football anytime soon, they also provided ample reason to keep reading until the novel's final sentence.

·

Sex.

To the teenaged male that I was when I first read *The Last Picture Show*, no other word conveyed as much mystery or caused such complicated feelings. There were times when I regarded the word with pure hatred. Why did the god whose existence I had not yet come to question have to invent such a thing? Look at all the trouble it caused. Men left their families over it. People killed one another over it. It distracted you from the truly important things in life, like executing a perfect trap block or delivering a good blindside hit on the other team's quarterback. What you had to do to even take part in the activity was silly and embarrassing. Furthermore, you knew your own parents must have done it at least once, which was terrible to contemplate.

Worst of all, I wasn't getting any. Why this should be so

was puzzling to me. My father had relented a little bit on the hair issue, so now mine looked pretty much like everyone else's. My face was at least average, and I brushed my teeth and used mouthwash and deodorant. As for my build, by the end of my junior year, I weighed 230 pounds and had a 31-inch waist. My stomach was flat, and my thighs and biceps rippled from all my weight training.

But this was the Bible Belt. And while murder might be the greatest sin of all, we never attended special assemblies to learn why it was wrong to kill. Yet every year, usually after the end of football season, when our minds began to wander, a day would come when the principal's voice suddenly crackled over the PA system. "I need all the girls to make their way down to gym for a special presentation." We knew what that meant. The girls' faces would blush, and as they rose from their desks, their eyes would be averted. If we were in class with one of the female teachers like, say, Mrs. H, she would keep her gaze trained on either the floor or the rear wall for the remainder of the period except when consulting the algebra text, which she knew backwards and forwards. If, on the other hand, we were in class with one of the male teachers like Coach S, he would snicker as soon as the girls' left the room, and for the rest of the period he would sit at the desk with his legs crossed and tell stupid jokes, which, I hasten to add, had nothing to do with sex. Many of the jokes concerned black people. It was that kind of school.

Shortly before the end of the period, the principal's

voice would again be heard, this time telling all the boys to leave and assemble at the doors on the east side of the gym. When the bell rang, the girls would exit the doors on the other side, and one of the coaches or the assistant principal would herd us through our designated doors like a bunch of bull yearlings. Coach R, who taught drivers' ed, a subject reserved for coaches who were too poorly prepared to handle something as tricky as history or civics, was especially stone-faced before these assemblies.

"Quit grab-assin'," he snarled at one of my classmates. "Learnin' about this stuff's the difference between a good life and the one you got now."

I required little convincing.

I was absent during the special assembly that all the guys agreed was probably the best of the bunch. It was delivered by a local physician, the father of a teammate; a couple of years down the road, when I sank into depression after the older woman I fell in love with quit having anything to do with me, he would recommend that I be checked into the state mental hospital. My father prevented this from happening, and I am grateful to him for that, as I was not and am not crazy. I don't hold the recommendation against the doctor, by the way. I was behaving very strangely, and he'd always been nice to me, just as he was when I saw him only a few months ago. He's in his eighties now. He quit watering the grass long enough to tell me hello and say he was proud of me.

When he delivered the sex talk, according to the friend

who described it, he began by confessing that he frequently had "wet dreams." My friend said he admitted he soaked the bed when this happened, and remarked that none of us should be ashamed when we had them too, because it was our bodies' way of getting rid of impulses that we should not give into at this stage of our lives.

The only one of these lectures that I remember well enough to describe was delivered by a traveling evangelist. (I remember thinking that if his life had worked out differently, perhaps my father would be called upon to deliver such presentations himself. What a treat that might have been.) The preacher's name has long since receded into the mists, but I recall him as a small man who was nearly bald and wore spectacles and a dark suit. I don't know exactly what he had said to the girls a few moments earlier, but I remember what he said to us, and I remember that he stood before a portable chalkboard near the center of the basketball court.

He raised the hand-held mic. "If I was to hand you a million dollars right now," he said, letting his eyes scan the east-side bleachers where all of us were sitting, "it wouldn't do you as much good as what I'm fixing to tell you."

He faced the chalkboard and drew a large, misshapen circle. Then he faintly shaded an area near the middle of the circle, and in the middle of the shaded area, he emphatically placed a dot. You could hear the impact of the chalk against the blackboard when he did it.

He turned back to us. "That's a woman's breast," he said.

A few of us dropped our heads to hide the grins that had dangerously appeared there, but nobody snickered. Coach R scanned the bleachers, ready to note any improper behavior.

"If a man wants to play with his wife's breast," our evangelist said, "there's not a thing in the world wrong with it. I'm not ashamed to tell you I play with my wife's sometimes." He walked closer to the bleachers. "But here's the thing, men—and I'm calling y'all men because that's what you're fixing to become. What's all right to do with your wife is not all right to do with anybody else. In fact, it's all wrong. Even if sweet little Sally Sue that you've been going with says okay, it's not. It's disrespectful, and it can lead to premature wedlock. It can even lead to prison. I've ministered to some men up there in Parchman, and I'm here to tell you it's a rough place to end up." He stepped back over to the chalkboard and stabbed at the breast with the chalk. "Getting too fixated on that at an early age can cost you your freedom. It can even cost you your life, and when you go to meet your maker it can land you someplace a lot worse than Parchman."

The Delta has always been especially good at repression. For most of the region's history, the two main targets of its well-honed skills have been black political activity and white premarital sex. The authority figures I looked up to were unconcerned about black sexual activity, as long as it did not involve a black man and a white woman. If black people slept around and created unwanted babies, it just confirmed a useful stereotype. If we did it, the social order was at risk. The initial sign of trouble, easily recognized by any watchful parent, was an act of masturbation.

I don't know if others recall the first time they practiced that ancient art or not, but I do. It was the day after I turned seven. While watching a morning rerun of *I Love Lucy* on the small portable TV in my bedroom, I began to stroke myself with a leftover party horn, one of those little paper coils that unrolls when you blow on it. Why I used that particular device, I have no idea. But actually putting my hand on my member for a reason other than steadying my aim as I stood near a toilet, I must have believed, would be to move beyond filthy into the territory of the truly vile.

At some point during that first session, I realized a little lubrication might be useful. So I decided to spit on the party horn. The problem was that if I brought it close to my mouth, my lips might inadvertently make contact with it, and it had touched the dirty part of me and, for all I knew, might result in disease. Fortunately, there were other leftover party horns.

Lest the reader think I am holding something back, I will go ahead and say it: seven-year-old Stevie Yarbrough loved Lucy, he thought she was beautiful and he wanted to see her naked. What good it would do him, he could not imagine, and he felt really bad about it. But the really-feeling-bad really made him happy. If this sounds confusing to you, rest assured that it confused him too.

In his meditation *Walter Benjamin at the Dairy Queen:*

Reflections on Sixty and Beyond, Larry McMurtry remarks that "the artists I have known best never give up anything—sex, rich food, Baby Ruths, Dr Pepper, opium." Whether I had artistic inclinations at the age of seven is open to question. But I was not about to give up my new pleasure, even if it resulted in eternal damnation.

In a couple of days, I ran out of uncontaminated party horns. I tried a few other objects—a Number Two lead pencil, a Chapstick, a Dr. Grabow pipe that belonged to my grandfather—but none of them worked as well. Finally, with a sense of resignation, I spit on my own fingers and took myself in hand.

Ever vigilant, my father wasted no time detecting my sin. How he realized I was doing it, I don't know, unless he observed me through the keyhole when I had the door closed. I think that unlikely, because he weighed around 220 pounds and sounded like a plow horse moving through the house. Regardless, one night he came into my room and shut the door. I was lying in bed reading *The Mystery of the Hooded Hawk* for the third or fourth time. It was supposedly too advanced for a boy my age, but I was apparently precocious in more ways than one. And yes, I really do remember what I was reading. Some experiences you never forget, and this was going to be one of them.

He sat down on the side of the bed, his bulk eliciting a strong protest from the box springs. "I need a word with you," he said.

The phrase *I need a word with you* never failed to chill

my heart. I laid the book face down on my chest. "Yes sir?"

"You know what happens," he asked, "when a boy starts to mess with that little thing between his legs?"

"No, sir," I said. I assumed he was going to tell me I had consigned myself to hell, but that didn't frighten me too badly because I had already heard Brother Joe say that God would forgive all our sins as long as we asked for His grace, and Brother Joe ought to know better than anyone else. I would ask for it the second my father rose and left the room. The only reason I hadn't already requested it was that I had no intention of quitting until forced to, and I knew it was wrong to pretend you were sorry if you weren't. If I never got discovered, I'd decided, I would wait until I was really old and close to death—around fifty, say—and then I would give it up and beg forgiveness. Clearly, though, I would have to adjust my timetable.

"What happens," my father said, "is that if a boy don't leave hisself alone down there, he gets where he can't pee."

"He *does*?" I squeaked.

"Sure enough. It's one of the worst things that can happen to a person." He pointed out the window in the general direction of the drainage ditch that had flooded the previous spring. "Think about what happens to the ditch out yonder," he said. "When it gets too full, why, it just throws all that nasty water into the fields and roads. But us men, we ain't made like that. When we get backed up, that pee don't have nowhere to go."

"What happens to it?" I cried.

"I don't even want to tell you. I'd hate to make you have nightmares. Bottom line is, as long as you leave yourself be, it won't happen."

While I was loath to confess, I needed some information immediately. "Is there any way to know if it's already happening to you?" I asked.

"Yeah. A boy's color gets real bad. He turns kind of yellow in the face. Fortunately, that ain't happened to you. You must be leaving that thing alone." He stood, told me to sleep well, and left my room, gently closing the door.

The fear did not leave the room when he did, however, as fear is among the most tenacious emotions. I shut my eyes and prayed hard, promising God all kinds of things. Not only would I never touch myself again, I would never again imagine Lucy or any other woman or girl with her clothes off. I would quit lying. I would never again say a curse word to myself just for the thrill the dirty word brought me. I'd quit watching football after church, keeping the Sabbath sacred. I would read the Bible every night and give up the Hardy Boys, and I would put my entire allowance in the collection plate each Sunday. I promised to give up everything that accorded me even the tiniest pleasure.

How long did my resolve last? My guess is maybe three weeks. Maybe even a month. When it finally deserted me, I became ever more stealthy, usually staging my sessions in the closet or even outside in the hayloft. The latter location added an additional element of fear to the endeavor, for we had found snakeskins up there and I could have lethal company.

Sex was linked to shame, secrecy, death and damnation. How many writers have been born of such trauma?

•

I have only spoken with Larry McMurtry once, in a telephone conversation that took place thirty-five years ago and lasted around ninety seconds. I called the DC area antiquarian book store that he operated in the early eighties, and he answered the phone. There were all sorts of things I intended to say, the first of which was how much his novels meant to me, especially *The Last Picture Show*. Something about his tone, which suggested that he had immediately intuited my reason for calling and was either very busy or, more likely, very tired of such calls, robbed me of all initiative. Instead, I stammered out a sentence or two about how I was thinking of writing my M.A. thesis on his work, and I wondered if he could help me obtain a copy of his novel *Leaving Cheyenne*, which the Ole Miss library did not possess and which I had been unable to find. The remainder of the conversation went something like this.

> *McMurtry: Are you looking for a first edition or just a reading copy?*
> *Me: A reading copy.*
> *McMurtry: It's being reissued next month by Penguin.*
> *Me: Oh. That's great.*
> *McMurtry: Goodbye, now.*

In other words, I don't know the author, and I have no personal basis for suggesting any similarities between his childhood and mine. Nor am I willing to commit the unpardonable fallacy of seeing him in either Sonny Crawford or Duane Moore. But in his essay "Eros in Archer County," from his 1968 collection *In a Narrow Grave: Essays on Texas*, McMurtry writes about his own discovery of sexual sensation:

> I was eight or nine years old, as I recall, and was climbing a street-sign pole. When I started up the pole I had no purpose in mind but casual exercise, but about the time I got to the top, the flexing activity that pole-climbing involves produced what I learned years later was an orgasm. I had not been expecting anything so delightful to happen at the top of that pole, and I hung for a moment in amazement before sliding down. A lady of my acquaintance happened to be standing nearby, so I hurried over and gave her an ecstatic report on the event. My description was probably rather vague, but I was able to pinpoint the area that felt so good, and that was enough for the lady. "Ssh," she said, looking apprehensively about. "Just don't tell anybody."

Like the young McMurtry, I absorbed the lesson, early on, that pleasure could only be enjoyed in hiding and at considerable risk, and I became a furtive creature. This obsession with sex and secrecy led to my earliest attempts to write fiction.

•

The first few years of my life, I'd had really bad asthma. A couple of times, after particularly violent bronchial seizures, I'd briefly stopped breathing. Being surrounded by cotton fields didn't help. In the summer and early autumn, when cropdusters swooped down over the house to loose streams of pesticides or the defoliant that would come to be known as Agent Orange, I was always sick. This kept me at home with my mother and grandmother and women from the community who dropped by from time to time. For weeks at a stretch, the only human beings I saw in the broad light of day were women whose ages ranged from around thirty to fifty.

I had legions of aunts. Sometimes, if they themselves weren't working and their husbands were, they came as well. As an only child frequently confined to the house, I was around them a lot, and it's fair to say two things: they fussed over me, and they didn't always take care to make sure their bodies were hidden from my eyes like they would have if I'd been a little older. Two of them in particular caught my imagination and held it. If I am to be truthful—and at the age of sixty, I don't see the need to be anything less—they still hold it, though one of them has been dead for years.

The younger of these two aunts was probably in her late twenties when I first laid eyes on her. She had dark hair that she wore fairly short and, though by no means fat, she verged on Rubenesque. She already had a houseful of children, most of whom were my age or a little older. She gave birth to her last when I was about five.

She and her family lived in another town, and for some reason that escapes me I was once left with them in the evening when the last of my cousins was a baby. While my aunt and uncle watched a television show, I played with my male cousins in their bedroom. At some point I needed to go pee. When I stepped into the living room, there sat my aunt on the couch beside my uncle. She had her blouse unbuttoned and was breast-feeding the baby. I had seen breasts before, but only because I managed to sneak a look, whereas she didn't even bother to hide the one that wasn't in use.

"I need to go to the bathroom," I said.

My aunt said she did too. She handed my cousin to my uncle, then pulled the halves of her blouse together but didn't button it. Standing, she took me by the hand and led me down the hall.

I assume I went ahead and relieved myself in her presence, but I don't remember. What I do remember is standing there and watching while she used a breast pump on herself. I don't remember what the breast pump looked like, whether it resembled the one my wife used nearly three decades later when we had our first daughter, nor do

I remember much about her breasts themselves, though I know they were larger than my mother's. What I do remember is that she closed her eyes while she was doing it, and that at some point during the process, she said, "Feels good, Stevie. Feels *real* good. This little pump's my lifesaver. I don't know what I'd do without it."

Over the next few years, whenever I saw her, my face and ears would begin to heat up, and even though my cousins always wanted to play and I was normally desperate to do it too, I tried to remain in whatever room she happened to be in. If she was shelling beans for supper, I'd offer to shell with her, and if she was washing dishes, I'd ask if I could dry them. My male cousins began to call me a sissy and, in one case, a pussy. She backhanded the one who called me that and then she grabbed a hunk of his hair and shoved him onto the porch and told him to go over to the "crick" and wash out his mouth. A few years later, after my uncle died an early death, she got married to another man, and I never saw her again, though I think about her often, how she closed her eyes and told a small boy, "Feels *real* good."

The other aunt was older, probably forty when I first took note of her, a tall, auburn-haired woman with broad shoulders and heavy hips. Though extremely religious, she had a wild streak. Periodically, she drank whiskey—a rarity among diehard Baptists—and she smoked like a diesel in need of a ring job. Like my other aunt, she had a house full of children, all of them girls, and her husband also died early. She married another man, and before long he died too. Toward the end of her life, she had cancer and, after I lost touch with her, I heard she had to have a leg amputated.

When I was around twelve or thirteen, both my mother and my grandmother came down with pneumonia. It was fall and picking time; my father had gone to work running a different gin, one owned by his brother, and my grandfather was working there as a yardman—a guy who drove a tractor all day and most of the night, pulling trailers onto the scales to be ginned, then pulling them to a distant corner of the gin yard where they waited until their owners came for them. Neither he or my father could afford to take off, and since my aunt wasn't working, she drove up from her home about a hundred miles away to look after me for a couple of days, feeding me and driving me to school. She preferred we stay at grandparents' house, which was just a mile down the road from ours. She'd stayed there many times and knew where everything was.

I was listening to a lot of rock music during those years, nearly always at my grandparents'. I couldn't risk it at home. My mom didn't mind, she actually liked a lot of it, especially Creedence Clearwater, but my father considered it evidence of all that was wrong in the country, and he'd forbidden it. Periodically, he would go through my record albums, and when he found anything that he considered unwholesome—which pretty much meant everything other than country or white gospel—he confiscated it. This was no small loss for me. Singles cost a dollar, albums around four dollars, and he had actually burned several of them.

Some time the first evening my aunt stayed with me, I asked her if I could listen to some music, making clear that I meant rock instead of country. She said sure, so I put something on, I don't recall what. While she washed dishes, I stood in a dark corner of the living room, doing what I always did when listening to rock. I pretended I was playing lead guitar, that I was onstage someplace like Madison Square Garden or the Royal Albert Hall, with my hair to my ass and banned substances in my blood. I mostly kept my eyes shut while I "played," so it surprised me when I opened them and saw my aunt standing there in the dark, with her hands on her hips and a grin on her face. "Yonna dance?" she asked, in her hill country brogue.

It occurs to me now that she may have been drinking, though I had seen no sign of a bottle, and I don't recall smelling anything on her breath except tobacco. "Sure," I said.

Whatever tune was playing must have been pretty lively, because she began to do the twist. She would have been about fifty by then, and the notion that a woman that age would know how to do something that I associated with youthful abandon all but made me swoon. What it didn't make me do was dance. I stood there watching her hips move from side to side, her breasts pushing against the fabric of her blouse.

When the tune ended, she regarded me with some odd mixture of amusement and concern. "You don't really know how to cut up, do you?"

I don't know what I said, how I reacted, whether or not her question hurt me, embarrassed me, made me angry, or simply made me wish it were not so obviously true.

"Let me show you," she said.

If this were a novel, I'd make the next tune a slow one. My aunt would step closer, so close I would smell the whiskey on her breath, and she would put her arms around me, and I would feel her breasts pressing against me, and those sensations would combine with the languid beat and our rhythmic motion to produce a physiological reaction in my poor tortured body. My aunt would become aware of it and she would either smile and tell me not to be ashamed, that it was a normal thing, or she would close her eyes and say something wistful, like I once made a character say in my novel *Prisoners of War* when she slow dances with her son: "'Lord, I'd forgotten what it's like to be with a boy your age. You always shut your eyes and make believe he's older.'" Something to acknowledge that the close proximity between an older woman and a young male relative can obliterate every last line but one.

But this is not a novel, and the next song on whatever record we were listening to was a burning rocker. She did make contact with me, grabbing me by my hands but keeping me at arm's length while forcing me to move my feet or be pulled off balance. She kept her eyes wide open, and I kept my eyes on her eyes, to avoid staring at her pulsating body. She was starting to perspire, her cheeks damp, her forehead too. "Uh, huh," she said. "Yeah."

When it was over, I could feel the pulse pounding in my throat. I'd worked up quite a sweat, moisture was trickling down my spine and under the waistband of my jockey shorts. To say that my heart was in riot would be to put it far too mildly. I lacked the language to say what I was feeling. I lack the language to say it even now, and so does everyone else.

How we got from that moment to the next one, I don't know, and there's no point in making it up. We may have watched TV for a while. Or maybe I did some homework, though generally I didn't bother, which could have explained why I was again failing algebra. Regardless, a couple of hours went by one way or another, and then we got ready for bed.

My grandparents slept in the same room but not in the same bed. They did have something that could serve as a guest room, but it was in the back half of the house, and since each room had only a space heater and neither of us had thought to turn that one on, we both slept in my grandparents' room. If this sounds too convenient, I can't help it. That's what happened.

Their beds did not stand side by side, which is probably a comment on how they lived their lives: the headboard of my grandfather's was flush against one wall, my grandmother's perpendicular to it, with just enough space between the mattresses for her to get in and out of bed. Neither of them was a reader—Nanny, as I called her, was completely blind in one eye and functionally illiterate—and they had no bedside lamps. So there was only the overhead to be dealt with, and I imagine my aunt was the one who switched it off.

I don't know if I had quit sleeping in pajamas by this time or not. I think I probably had, and I suspect that the instant the light went out, I seized the opportunity to leap out of everything but my underwear and cover myself head to toe. Through the darkness, I could see her standing five or six feet away. She had her back to me, and I couldn't tell how much she was taking off. I hoped I would wake up first, so that if she was sleeping without a top I might get a look at her bare shoulders and breasts, but that didn't happen, largely because I lay awake half the night and only woke when she ran a finger along my chin the next morning and said, "Hey, time to rise and shine." By then she was fully dressed.

When she got into bed that night, the first thing she did was light a cigarette. The orange glow waxed and waned with her puffs. As my eyes adjusted to the darkness, I could see she had propped herself up on a couple of pillows, but it looked like she'd pulled the covers up over everything of great interest to me.

"You don't smoke, do you?" she asked.

"No ma'am."

"Ever drunk a beer?"

"No ma'am."

"Well, good for you. Best thing's not to start down either road. I wish I hadn't. But sometimes . . . well, sometimes."

I waited for her to say more, but she didn't. She finished that cigarette, and a few minutes later she lit another. I lay there watching the orange glow growing brighter, then fainter, then brighter once more. I'm not sure how many she smoked. Maybe three. Maybe four. After a while the sound of her breathing changed, and the springs squeaked as she rolled onto her side. Before long, it began to rain, big drops beating down on the tin roof, and the next thing I knew she was running her finger over my chin, telling me it was time to get up and face the day.

•

Writers, I have told three decades worth of students, write about the things they can't get off their minds. I speak from the depths of my own experience.

I used lined paper ripped from a spiral notebook. Pen or pencil, I don't recall. Let's say it was a Bic ballpoint. But not one of those thinline jobs, because what I wrote was bold and, to put it mildly, lacking nuance. It also lacked authority, as I had no experience to build on and was relegated to the realm of my own impoverished imagination.

In the first of my efforts, it was just the older of my two aunts and me. She had come to stay with me, and we had danced, just as we did in reality. That lasted for maybe a paragraph. In the second paragraph, she produced a bottle of whiskey, and I like to think that I lent at least a fragment of authenticity by naming the brand. If so, I probably said Old Crow, because my father had begun to drink, quite heavily, and that was his preference. My narrator—for I wrote in the first person—took a couple of swigs and threw caution to the winds. (This would prove a realistic touch. Bourbon, I am sorry to say, has always emboldened me.) To his aunt, my newly intrepid character said something along the lines of "Would you explain to me how to go about having sex?"

Matter-of-factly, the narrator's aunt provided a detailed description of cunnilingus, which I guarantee you I misspelled, and then she said that after the man did that to the woman, she would do it to him. (I knew there was a specific word for this activity too, but I could not remember it and would not have wasted time looking it up.) After that, she said, the woman would lie on her back and the man would "go to town in her."

"I don't suppose," my narrator said, trying to act nonchalant, "you'd let me do that with you?"

For a moment, she considered his request. "Well," she said, taking a swig of the whiskey, then beginning to unbutton her blouse, "let's don't tell nobody." I still recall the last line of this three-page vignette: "Then I passed out with my kindhearted aunt's big nipple in my mouth."

Because I wanted to be fair to my other aunt, who after all had entered my fantasies first, a day or two later I wrote one involving her. Then I decided What the hell, why not go for broke and write one about the three of us?

For the next couple of weeks, I was a veritable Georges

Simenon. Though I always returned to my aunts, I spread my attention to several of the teachers at my school, as well the mothers of various classmates. I experimented with different settings and situations. In one of them I was hospitalized with a high fever. My biology teacher, who'd been transformed into a nurse, pulled her clothes off and climbed in beside me, noting that the best way to get rid of a fever was to exercise it out of your body, which she helped me do. I wrote encounters that occurred in a cotton trailer, under the Sunflower River bridge while a tornado raged above, in the football team's whirlpool. In each of them I was young and inexperienced, and my partners found great joy in showing me the ropes. In retrospect, I'm sure the heavily censored version of *The Graduate* that had been shown on network TV fueled some of these fantasies, as did the hit tune "Mrs. Robinson," which I had all but worn out on our record player.

The problem, of course, was what to do with all the pages I'd written. I could not bring myself to destroy them. After all, if I ever developed writers' block, which seemed unlikely, they could be "reused." Since my father often prowled through my belongings, these little vignettes would have to be carefully hidden, and I decided the safest place to tuck them away was inside a few record albums. As long as he didn't see anything by a rock group, he'd leave them along. He almost never listened to music.

But one night, when I was down at my grandparents' house, he apparently imbibed a good bit of whiskey, started feeling maudlin and decided he needed to hear Hank Williams. When my grandfather dropped me off at our house, he must have just made his discovery: my mother met me at the front door, and her face was as white as the paper on which I had written my first words of fiction. She managed to move her lips, but no words emerged.

"What's the matter?" I asked. All she could do was turn toward the hallway.

"*Get in here!*" I heard him holler from my room. "Get the hell in here right now!"

•

I was once on an airplane that had to turn around mid-flight and return to the Dallas–Fort Worth airport after a passenger issued a series of threats against the crew and other passengers. During the fifteen or twenty minutes we remained airborn, before the doors burst open and a team of officers pulled the man from his seat and dragged him unceremoniously away, I was terribly frightened. But my fear could not compare to what I felt as I plodded down the hallway to face my fate.

Have you ever seen a big man hyperventilate? It's an impressive if harrowing sight. Perhaps because his brain was oxygen-deprived, his face had devolved beyond red to the nether side of purple. In his left hand he held the only record album he truly loved, a selection of country gospel tunes by the Chuckwagon Gang. From his right hand dangled the pages he had found inside the album: the little piece about the threesome with my aunts. Other albums and manuscripts were strewn about the floor.

"Shut . . ." he began, then paused to gasp for air. "Shut . . . the . . . fucking . . . door."

I had never heard him say any form of the word *fuck* before. I suspect it came so readily to mind because while my first couple of pieces were written in comically sterile language—"Let's go ahead now and have a little intercourse"—the later ones called a spade a fucking spade.

I observed my own hand as it moved erratically toward the doorknob. Parkinson's could not have exerted a greater effect on my motor skills at that moment. I figured I was about to be beaten half to death. Turning to face him, I tried to gauge the chances of throwing myself onto the bed and then diving through the window. The glass would cut me badly and might even sever my jugular, but on the whole it would probably be less painful than what I was about to suffer.

"You . . . you. . . ." He shook his head, then raised the manuscript and fanned his face with it.

I decided offering a prompt might be in my own best interest. "I didn't actually do any of those things," I said. "I was just making them up. It was all fiction. You know, like Ernest Hemingway or somebody."

"Somebody," he said, "like Ernest Hemingway."

"I think I want to be a writer. And you have to be able to write about all sorts of things." It occurred to me that an additional comment might aid my cause. "Even things you haven't done. You have to be able to tap your imagination."

"And you've tapped yours, have you?"

"Yes sir. I didn't like having to do it. It made me , , , it made me feel unclean. But I was practicing. I'm willing to work for what I want."

He batted his thigh with the account of my little familial threesome. Looking back, I feel certain he was revising his opinion of me, that he'd never realized what a creative liar he had raised. If my mother was an open book, I was a closed book, one with plenty of interesting subtext. Had he set out to parse me, imagine how many footnotes and marginal notations might have been required. It might even have brought him as much pleasure as writing those sermons.

I could not help but feel proud of myself. In that moment, I first began to grasp that the world might be full of possibility, even for a boy who lived in a house like mine and had never been more than four hundred miles from the place where he was born. I felt it probable, if not quite certain, that I would one day see New York, maybe even LA. I would lie my way right out of the cotton fields and into Central Park.

His face was beginning to look less stormy. "This is vile, nasty stuff you wrote here," he said. "Lord, it's disgusting. And it ain't realistic neither." His shook his head, and for an instant it seemed he was fighting the urge to smile. If so, he mastered it. "These literary efforts," he said, waving the manuscript at me, then gesturing at those strewn across the floor, "I'm fixing to burn 'em. Now as soon as I leave this room, you turn out the light and you get in that bed." He gathered up all the pages and tucked them under his arm. I feel as confident as I've ever felt about anything that he did not burn them, that he took them out and reread them from time to time, marveling at the unfiltered imagination of the young man he had sired. For many years I harbored the fear that they would somehow resurface.

Upon reaching the door, he turned and fired a parting shot. "By the way," he said, "when you get under them covers, don't you dare mess with yourself. Any minute I'm liable to come check."

THE PLOT OF *THE LAST PICTURE SHOW* REVOLVES AROUND three "older" women, with each of whom young Sonny Crawford achieves a degree of intimacy. He gets to sleep with two of them, though neither of those would have been his first choice. The only one of the trio who doesn't end up in bed with him is the waitress at Sam the Lion's all-night café, Genevieve Morgan, who is without question the most grounded. Though her husband has been seriously hurt in an oil field accident and, as she tells Sonny, they have so many medical bills that she will "'probably be making cheeseburgers for your grandkids,'" she's morally centered without being sanctimonious and is basically accepting of her situation.

The introduction of Genevieve, in the novel's third chapter, galvanized my interest just as I was starting to think about closing the book. "She was a shapely black-headed woman in her mid-thirties," McMurtry writes, "[who] was beginning to thicken a bit at the waist, but she was still pretty, high-breasted, and long-legged." Genevieve works a nightshift from ten until six, and in the wee hours of the morning, after he finishes making butane deliveries for his boss Frank Fartley, Sonny Crawford finds himself alone with her. She tells him if he'll come keep her company in the back while she washes dishes, she'll give him a piece of pie. He is only too willing, just as I would have been, to do as she asks. Like a lot of the local boys, Sonny has a serious crush on her, a fact of which she's well-aware, but she never makes an effort to exploit it, treating him with unfailing kindness and concern, acting, one might even say, like a surrogate mother.

One of the other two older women, Ruth Popper, is married to the local high school football coach. Football coaches, in my own experience, lend themselves easily to caricature because they live in an Us vs. Them world: there are folks in the right uniforms and folks in the wrong ones. It's a militaristic mindset, all about taking ground and holding it, imposing your will on others. McMurtry makes brutal sport of Ruth's husband Herman Popper, revealing that he's about as adept at caricature as Flannery O'Connor.

When the coach first appears on the page, he's wearing a green fatigue jacket that he stole from the army, and we're told that he's a huge man with an enormous gut. During football games he prowls the sidelines, making faces at the officials, and at basketball practice he sits on a bridge chair, where he chews tobacco and continuously scratches his genitals. He enjoys harassing Joe Bob Blanton, the preacher's son, whose sexual equipment, he claims, is insufficient. Because he appears to think of little besides sex and because his favorite saying is "'Find 'em, fool 'em, fuck 'em and forget 'em,'" all his charges assume he's a relentless letch.

The only person who knows otherwise is his wife. Ruth is a small, weary-looking woman, though Sam the Lion tells Sonny and Duane that when she was young she was beautiful. At Christmas she bakes cookies and brings them to the two boys, but otherwise she is seldom seen around town. People assume she's worn out by trying to satisfy her husband's sexual needs and that the necessity for rest is what keeps her out of the public eye.

In fact, she and the coach have virtually no sexual relationship at all. The only time we ever see them having sex, the coach's desire has been kindled not by his wife but by his anger at an attractive female student named Jacy Farrow, whom he blames for distracting Duane and keeping him from focusing on athletics.

Lying in bed, the coach keeps thinking about Jacy, "how nice it would be to hump a little rich girl like her until she got so sick of it she would never want to see another boy, much less bother one." While entertaining these thoughts, he happens to notice his wife, who always undresses behind the closet door. When she steps from behind it, pulling on her nightgown, he tells himself that while he will never get a shot at Jacy, Ruth is right there. Suddenly excited, the coach rises, walks over to his sock drawer, pulls out a condom and goes into the bathroom to prepare himself. Then he turns out the light, heads back to bed, rolls on top of his wife and begins to go at her "athletically."

Reviewers have rightly praised McMurtry's ability to write believable women characters, and this has never been more memorably displayed than in the passage that follows, as the narrative perspective shifts to Ruth.

> Her chest and abdomen felt crushed. . . . What was crushing her was the weight of all the food she had fed Herman through the years, all the steaks, all the black-eyed peas, all the canned peaches. It was particularly the canned peaches: she had never until that moment realized how much she hated them. It seemed to her that pyramids of cans of slimy peaches piled on her abdomen. After a moment the weight became intolerable and she moved a little, to try and ease it. . . . As she kept moving . . . she became aware of a distant pleasure. She began to writhe a little.

Her attempts surprise and outrage the coach. It's indecent, he thinks. He tries "to beat Ruth down with his body," but he can no more stop her frenzied movements than he can stop his own.

Far from being pleased, the coach is appalled by his wife's orgasm, especially when she clamps her legs together to keep him from withdrawing. As soon as she relaxes, he hurries to the bathroom to wash himself off, thinking how messy women's bodies are.

The reader is armed with two pieces of knowledge that Coach Popper lacks. The first is that he is a latent gay, who might have been much happier if he could have been with a man, preferably a very young one like the boy who currently plays quarterback for the football team. The second is that Ruth has already begun an affair with Sonny Crawford.

•

It is difficult to talk about *The Last Picture Show* as a novel without also discussing the far more widely appreciated film version. The movie was directed by Peter Bogdanovich, and he co-wrote the script with McMurtry, who has said that the director forced him to depict Sonny in a more sympathetic light. There are a number of reasons to think this is probably true. In an interview at the end of the special edition DVD release of the director's cut, Bogdanovich talks about softening Duane's character by casting the affable Jeff Bridges in that role. And while he doesn't explicitly state his reasons for choosing Timothy Bottoms to play Sonny, at the time the film was made Bottoms was nineteen years old, with thick wavy hair and large, sad eyes. He had previously appeared in only the film version of Dalton Trumbo's novel *Johnny Got His Gun,* and under the skillful direction of Bogdanovich he achieves a markedly unaffected performance as an ordinary boy who doesn't expect or ask much of life.

Ruth Popper is played by Cloris Leachman, a former runner-up in the 1946 Miss America pageant. Leachman won an Oscar as Best Supporting Actress, and her portrayal of Ruth is masterful. In both the book and the film, her affair with the much younger man is inadvertently set in motion by Coach Popper, who asks Sonny if he can drive her over to see the doctor in Olney, explaining that she's been sick and is afraid they might need to give her drugs that would make it unsafe for her to drive. He promises to get Sonny out of afternoon classes if he'll run the errand that the coach clearly considers as, at best, a nuisance.

Though I have read the novel seven or eight times and like to think I know the book quite well, I have probably seen the film close to fifteen times. And it amazed me, when I reread the book immediately before beginning this project, how much of what I thought I knew about Sonny and Ruth's affair is drawn not from the book itself but from the film.

When the movie began shooting, Leachman was forty-two years old. But the first time we see her, she looks a good ten or even fifteen years older, her hair up in a bun, her face thin and ascetic, its paleness further accentuated by the director's controversial decision to film in black and white. Everything but her face is covered. She's wearing a long grayish coat and a dark hat. She's as un-sexual a being as one could imagine.

The initial description of her in the novel is markedly different. As Sonny drives her to Olney, she stares out the window, giving him a chance to observe her without being noticed. "Her hair was brown with just a few traces of gray, and she wore it long, almost shoulder length. There was something about her that was really pretty. She was a little too thin, and her skin was too fair for the country she lived in: wind and sun freckled her on her cheekbones and beneath her eyes."

In the film Sonny takes little note of her, biding his time until he can drive her back home, at which point she suddenly invites him inside for a Dr Pepper. As he starts to drink it, she bursts into tears. Though uncomfortable, he offers up a few platitudes, suggesting that she will probably be glad when basketball season ends so the coach can be home more often. This remark causes Ruth to observe, "You don't know a thing about it, do you?" (The word "it" is allowed to remain divorced from its antecedent, in one of the film's few concessions to the mores of the early seventies. The novel is much more direct about the coach's repressed homoerotic inclinations.) Sonny leaves without out even the slightest suggestion of an attraction having formed. If anything, he seems to find Ruth repulsive.

What happens in the novel, while arguably more dramatic, is significantly less nuanced. Ruth cries all the way home from the doctor's office, prompting Sonny to ask if she'd like him to take her to the hospital. Instead she asks him to come inside for a soft drink and cookies, and once more, she begins to cry, this time violently. Sonny thinks that she is surely crazy, and he wants to get away from her, which Ruth seems to sense. She eventually manages to stop and wipe her face. Then she rises, steps closer and puts her hand against his cheek.

The remainder of the scene is nothing if not blunt. Ruth admits she would like to seduce him and asks if he has a girlfriend, and he reveals that he has recently broken up with a girl that he didn't like very much anyway. "'I already like you,'" he tells Ruth, "'better than I liked her.'" The comment brings a smile to her face, and though she soon sends Sonny away, the reader has every expectation that before long the two of them will end up in bed. Sixty pages later they do.

Their affair, begun in winter, lasts through the spring, their afternoon trysts conducted on a quilt in the bedroom Ruth shares with Coach Popper. The relationship, predictably, means different things to each of them. Because he enjoys the sex, Sonny is willing to let her love him, though he finds it "strange" and it takes a while for him to accept her affection. Initially the sex is not quite satisfactory for Ruth—sex, we learn, never has been—but she is terrified that Sonny will stop coming to see her. So she does everything possible to make him comfortable, preparing hot chocolate for him and mending his clothes, performing the functions of both lover and mother. Eventually, she experiences a sexual "breakthrough," and they become more at ease with each other. The affair, of course, is destined to end badly, in the process doing a lot more damage to Ruth than it will to her young lover.

•

The remaining older woman who enters Sonny's life is Lois Farrow, the wife of the wealthiest man in town, who struck it rich in the oil business. Cynical, bitter, smart and attractive, Lois is the mother of Jacy Farrow, the girl every boy at the high school is dying to win. When the novel opens, Jacy is going steady with Sonny's best friend Duane, much to the consternation of her mother, who wastes no opportunity to break them up.

We first meet Lois at a party her husband Gene has thrown at his ranch for his employees. At the time, Duane is working for him, so he invites Sonny along. Lois is drinking whiskey and shooting craps, and she loses six hundred dollars to Abilene and tries to make her husband Gene fire him. When Gene refuses, she subjects him and Abilene to a cussing, then jumps in her Cadillac and promptly drives into a tree. Unhurt, she climbs out and walks off toward town.

Nothing less than a tree or a wall is capable of stopping Lois, and everybody seems to know it, particularly her husband. Theirs, we deduce, is a loveless marriage, and the glue that binds them together is money. Lois likes to spend it. "'I scared your daddy into getting rich,'" she tells her daughter, Jacy. "'He's so scared of me that for twenty years he's done nothing but run around trying to find things to please me. He's never found the right things but he made a million dollars looking.'" Though she comes off as brusque, if not outright harsh, she possesses plenty of worldly wisdom, and she is not without concern for Jacy. She warns her that life is essentially an exercise in boredom, that we do the same things time after time and that the fastest way for her to get bored half to death would be to marry Duane.

Lois has slept with Abilene, though she appears to despise him now, and later in the book we learn that some twenty years ago, when she was already married to Gene, she had a fling with Sam the Lion. It's one of those things that all the adults in town know but nobody talks about, and when Sam tells Sonny about it on a fishing trip with Billy, he is careful not to name the young woman he once brought to the same fishing tank, where they went swimming nude. If she were there right now, he confesses, he'd probably again be just as smitten. He goes on to deliver one of the best lines in the novel: "'Being crazy about a woman like her's always the right thing to do.'" Later, after Sam has a stroke and dies, Sonny notices Lois weeping profusely at the burial ceremony. He asks Genevieve if she was the lover Sam told him about, and the waitress confirms it, remarking that Lois Farrow was once the liveliest person in town.

How can Sonny Crawford resist Lois when the opportunity presents itself?

When his affair with Ruth ends, Lois's daughter Jacy is the reason. After ditching Sonny's friend Duane for a rich boy in Wichita Falls, who in turn ditches her, Jacy decides Sonny might provide some summer fun. So she cold-bloodedly sets out to take him away from Ruth—and yes, the entire town, with the exception of Coach Popper himself, knows all about the affair. Once Jacy beckons, Sonny drops Ruth with little remorse. After causing a fight between him and Duane that leaves Sonny temporarily blind in one eye, Jacy talks him into eloping to Oklahoma. Before departing, she pens her parents a note telling them precisely where she and Sonny plan to get married. It's notoriety she craves, and it's clear to the reader, if not to Sonny, that she hopes her folks will put a stop to things before she ever has to spend her wedding night with him.

She is not disappointed. Her parents track the two of them down in Oklahoma, and her father orders her into the car with him, telling Sonny that for all he cares, he can walk all the way back to Thalia. Instead, Lois offers him a ride home in Jacy's car. On their way, something that has always seemed to me a little too predictable happens. To my mind, it's the single most significant difference between the novel and the film.

Lois begins musing about Sam the Lion, telling Sonny that "'he was the only man in that whole horny town who knew what sex was worth. . . . I probably never would have learned myself if it hadn't been for Sam. I'd be one of those Amity types who thinks bridge is the best thing life offers womankind.'" She becomes more and more emotional, then suddenly pulls onto the side of the road, slides across the seat and throws herself into Sonny's arms. Then she eases her hand inside his shirt.

Calm now, she tells Sonny that while he may or may

not know what she's worth, she likes him and would like to make sure that he has a much nicer wedding night than he would have experienced with her daughter. She drives to a motel, pays for a room, and they go inside and he watches, captivated and more than a little frightened, as she undresses. She is well aware of his fear. What follows is some of the most evocative writing in the novel:

> She kissed him and played with him until he began to play too. He relaxed and became as serious and playful as she was. She seemed really glad to be with him, crazy as it was. What surprised him most was the lightness of her movement . . . she seemed weightless, so light and easy that they might have been floating together. He came right away, without remembering her at all, and it was only a little later, when he did remember, that he wondered if he had come too soon. . . .
>
> "You've got a big inferiority complex you ought to cure yourself of," she said.
>
> A little later she spoke again. "It's not how much you're worth to the woman," she said quietly. "It's how much you're worth to yourself."

As much as I like the writing in this scene and the one that occurs when Lois lets Sonny out in Thalia at dawn, I've always preferred what happens in the film. Though it's clear a connection between Lois and Sonny has been made, they never stop at a motel: instead, they park before the poolhall, which Sam has left Sonny in his will and where Sonny now lives with Billy. There, they discuss Sam, and Lois speaks several of the lines from the novel that I've previously quoted, including the one about how terrible it is to find only one man who knows what "you"—as opposed to "it," namely, sex—are worth. Drunk on the bourbon Lois gave him, Sonny tells her that he can see why Sam liked her. Lois, played beautifully by Ellen Burstyn, responds that she can also see what Sam must have seen in Sonny. They exchange a long, silent look, during which the film's original audience must have expected they were about to head into the poolhall and throw their clothes off. Then Lois says, simply, "No. Think I'll go on home."

·

It's the fully-grown, adult version of Steve Yarbrough who prefers certain aspects of the film to those in the book. The seventeen-year-old who read the novel was deeply disappointed when he finally got to see the movie—not in the theater, I hasten to add, because the theater in my hometown, as I mentioned earlier, had already shut down. Instead, I saw it on network TV, and while a few things had been edited out, in the main it was the film as we know it today. Much of what attracted me to the novel was gone. The sex scenes, needless to say, depicted no naked coupling, whereas the book laid it all out there. When Sonny and Ruth kissed for the first time, behind the American Legion Hall where a Christmas dance was in progress, it seemed oddly unbelievable, because none of the dialogue that preceded the event in the novel was in the film. They just looked at each other and were suddenly kissing passionately. The boy that I was didn't know things like that just happened, whereas the man I am knows that they sometimes do, if not often enough, and that such moments should be savored and only analyzed later, if at all.

My aesthetic preference, developed over a lifetime, is usually for the subtle flanking movement rather than the frontal assault. I don't question for a second, though, that in places as drab and numbing as Thalia, people's desperation occasionally drives them to do dangerous things, and that women trapped in bad marriages like Ruth and Lois sometimes offer themselves to lost boys like Sonny Crawford.

LET'S SAY SHE WORKED AT THE PUBLIC LIBRARY. WE'LL make her Miss LuAnn's younger colleague. A woman of thirty-six when I'm eighteen, she presumably knows twice as much about the world as I do by virtue of having lived in it twice as long. Let's say she has reddish-brown hair and a pale complexion, that she's of average height and weight, that she always wears a dress or a nice skirt and blouse. Even if you run into her in one of the aisles at the Piggly Wiggly or its competitor, the Sunflower Food Store, you will not see her wearing jeans. She'll always have on a nice pair of shoes, too, something "sensible," as I used to hear them described.

She's married, of course. She has a little girl, whom we'll assign the age of eight, so that she's a perfect decade younger than I am. We'll make her husband a local insurance agent, a graduate of the University of Southern Mississippi, where he played shortstop on the baseball team. A few years older than his wife, he just turned forty. He's a deacon at First Baptist, the picture of Christian rectitude.

Except for one thing.

Two years ago, while serving as a volunteer coach at the all-white private school, he became infatuated with a member of the girl's softball team. Exactly what passed between them is open to question, but one day he came home and told his wife that he was in love with the girl and that he was considering leaving her. In the end, this didn't happen. He prayed and he prayed, and he consulted his minister and a couple of the other deacons whose discretion he trusted, and all of them assured him that if he took this terrible step, he could no longer serve the Lord, that he would be out of fellowship for the remainder of his days. God, he finally told both the girl and his wife, just would not let him do it. It simply was not His will.

The first conversation we ever have concerns the football team. Like virtually every white person in town, she's a fan. She never misses a game. "That was an important tackle you made down on the goal line the other night," she says.

She pronounces the word "other" as *oth-uh*. An "r" on the end of a word has about as much chance with her, I will discover, as it would with a white working-class Bostonian. In the context of the Delta, though, hers is the aristocratic accent, whereas mine identifies me as the son of working-class parents. I've only recently quit placing an "r" on the ends of words like "Alabama" and "lasagna."

I know, of course, who she is. I've been seeing her around town my whole life, and once or twice she's silently stamped the books I checked out. Her husband, whom we'll call Pete Simmons, carries the insurance on our car and truck as well as our house, and every year or so he stops off to go over the policy with my dad. I've formed the impression, based on no hard evidence, that my father doesn't like him. It could be nothing more than the fact that he drives a nicer automobile than ours, has a college degree and lives in a nice house. Or it could be nothing at all. Later, when Mr. Simmons threatens to take a gun to me, my father will begin to drive by their house, his 9 mm. clamped between his legs. Later still, when my first book comes out with a story about a football player who falls in love with an older woman, my father will tell me that it was not Mr. Simmons he was thinking of shooting. It was his wife instead. She will never know, he will say, just how close she came to dying. He almost killed her one night when I was in the hospital, full of some drug that kept me so sedated I couldn't get out of bed and go call her. She was standing in her driveway, getting ready to climb in her car, and she never noticed him when he slowly drove by. He was a good marksman. He would not have missed.

She needs a name. Let's call her Jane.

That day in the library, she's still Mrs. Simmons. She's been shelving books near where I'm browsing, pulling them off a metal cart and placing them in the proper spot. After complimenting the play I made, she asks what I'm planning to read.

Odds are, it's some kind of suspense novel. I liked *The*

Last Picture Show, but now I'm back in the mood for various types of mayhem: murder, spies, war. Leon Uris is always a good bet to deliver all of that and much more. I show her the book.

"*Topaz*," she says. "That's not one of his better ones." *Bett-uh*.

"It's the only one I haven't read."

"I noticed," she says, "that you've checked out quite a few of his. Some of them two or three times. Is he your favorite writer?" *Write-uh*.

This is probably the point at which I begin to feel slightly flattered. It's not that I'm unused to positive attention. I'm getting a lot of it these days. I can't go anywhere without someone telling me I made a great open-field block on that sweep, or that they loved the blindside hit I laid on Lee Academy's quarterback—"It's a wonder that boy got up"— or that Ole Miss sure could use me, Lord Amighty could they ever. Much, but not all, of that attention comes from men around town. Some of it comes from their wives. But all of it concerns football. None of them ever asks what book I'm reading, what records I've been listening to, what I plan to do when I grow up. Those things don't matter. To all the white adults in town, I'm a football player, period. Big number 72.

I don't know how I know how to talk to a woman like her, but I seem to. I tell her that Uris probably is my favorite writer, right now at least, and then I ask who hers is. It's a simple enough question, but it's also one that I would not have posed a year ago. The many differences between her and me would have left me tongue-tied. Rather than meeting her gaze, I would have stared at the floor.

"All things considered," she says, "it's probably Carson McCullers."

I have never heard of Carson McCullers, and it doesn't occur to me that Carson could be a woman's name. "What's his best book?" I ask.

She makes a decision, which she will tell me about some months from now: she elects not to inform me that the author is a woman. Somehow, she knows that it would embarrass me to have my misconception corrected, that despite frequently being yelled at by coaches and responding by hitting my opponents just a little bit harder next time, I am intellectually insecure, ashamed of my bad grades and unworldly nature. I've never even been to New Orleans, for Christ's sake. "This is McCullers' best," she says, pulling a book off the shelf.

The dust jacket is missing, and the title holds little or no appeal for me, but it seems wrong not to flip through the book. I read the first few sentences, which describe how each morning "two mutes" leave the house they live in and walk together to work. I have absolutely no interest in reading another word of it, and I won't until three years from now, after I quit playing football and transfer to Ole Miss to major in English and philosophy. But I tuck the book under my arm with the Leon Uris novel.

"You'll let me know what you think when you finish it?" she asks, as if what I think actually matters.

"Yes ma'am," I tell her.

She steps back over to the cart and again begins shelving books, and though I know I should quit standing there looking at her, it's as if my feet are stuck to the floor. There is nothing unusual about her: she's average in every way, and today, as if to accentuate her lack of singularity, she has worn an aggressively nondescript beige dress. Though I've fantasized about many of the older women I've seen around town, she has never been among them. Until this moment, the thought never crossed my mind. But from today on, it will be there all the time.

·

The season concludes, my team losing the AAA Academy Conference (read: all-white) championship game 13-0. I play terribly, overpowered and outclassed by a lineman who's two inches taller, twenty pounds heavier, stronger, quicker: just better. Next year he'll be playing in the SEC, making tackles against Alabama and LSU, while I'll be riding the bench in the Gulf South Conference, not even gracing the field against such powerhouses as UT Martin and Livingston State. I am, in other words, pretty much where Sonny Crawford finds himself as *The Last Picture Show* opens. The final high school game is over, and my usefulness to the town is too.

Most people don't stop being who they were overnight. But if your identity is as dependent on the opinion of others as mine was, it can happen with shocking speed, and for me it did. When I stopped by the local diner the next day for a hamburger and Coke, several men were in there eating lunch. A few of them looked up as I entered, then quickly looked away, and nobody said a word to me except the owner, a man who for the past couple of years had acted like the governor had shown up each time I walked through the door. That day he wouldn't meet my gaze, just asked me what I wanted and, as he turned to clip the slip on the order wheel, muttered, "You got your butt kicked all over the field last night."

When he came over and slapped my burger on the table, I ate with my head down, my face on fire. I got out of there as fast as I could. It was a cold rainy Saturday, and I spent the remainder of the day driving around town or traversing back roads, trying to come to terms with my new reality. I no longer mattered. I might never matter again.

With nothing to do on Monday afternoon when I normally would have been at football practice or lifting weights with the rest of the team to prepare for the following season, I went to the library, and there she was at the circulation desk, checking books out to an elderly couple. She glanced up and smiled, but otherwise ignored me. I'd brought back *The Heart Is a Lonely Hunter*, as well as *Topaz*, which I hadn't liked all that much. I waited until the old folks left before walking up to the desk and handing her the books. "You're right," I said. "This McCullers guy can really write."

As a student at Southern Mississippi, I would learn, she had taken part in a number of drama productions and knew a little bit about acting. She understood that I hadn't read the book. But rather than asking what I liked about it—which, since I had no acting ability at all, might have forced me to stammer and hang my head, possibly never to return—she maintained a straight face and asked my opinion of the Uris novel.

I told her I'd found the plot predictable and thought the book lacked the level of detail Uris always mustered when he wrote about the South Pacific, or the Holocaust, or the Middle East. "I don't think he's been to Cuba," I said.

"So you think writers need to visit a particular place before they write about it?"

"Yes ma'am. I mean, that makes sense to me. If they want to make it seem realistic."

"What about science fiction?"

Rather than tell her that I didn't read science fiction, I said, "If a place doesn't exist, you can't be wrong when you write about it. You can just make up anything."

"What about historical fiction? Somebody once said that the past is always a foreign country. The writer of a novel about ancient Greece can't really go there. All he can do is go to modern-day Greece, and that's not the same place."

I did not think, as I stood there, that I was engaged in the first semi-intellectual conversation of my life, or that I was setting forth a fairly rigid set of aesthetic preferences which, probably to my own detriment, would not change significantly over the next forty years. Instead, I was wishing that the white sweater she wore did not completely cover her shoulders. I wondered if the skin there was the same shade as her face. "It's still the same landscape," I said. "It's still got the same rivers and mountains."

A middle-school girl walked up with an armload of books. "It's a shame you didn't come by sooner," Mrs. Simmons told me, as she reached for the date stamp. "I always take a coffee break around 3:15 and, if the weather's good, I like to sit in that little garden out back. We could have discussed this longer. I find it interesting."

•

I've always been a pretty good liar. It's a skill my poor mom helped me develop at an early age. When I was eight or nine, she used to take me with her to Memphis, where we could shop for cheaper groceries, then swing by Graceland and hang out at the gates for a while with others hoping for a glimpse of Elvis. She never failed to caution me, "Don't tell your Daddy where we went after the grocery store," and I never did. Nor did I tell him when we ate lunch at a place called the Crystal Grill on shopping trips to Greenwood—she always had the vegetable plate, which cost only a dollar, and I had baked ham for $1.85. In there, on Saturdays, we occasionally saw a man named Byron De La Beckwith, who had been acquitted of murdering Civil

Rights Leader Medgar Evers but would be convicted of the crime thirty years later, after new evidence emerged. My childhood, it comes to me now, not for the first time, was all but guaranteed to create a skilled prevaricator, if not a novelist. Everything and everyone was writ large, and next to nothing could be admitted without possibly serious consequences.

After the end of my senior season, I concocted various lies, often without a moment's lead time, to explain where I went in the afternoons, telling my dad that I'd driven over to the Winterville Indian Mounds, so that I could run to the top and back one hundred times in an effort to increase my lung capacity. I told him one of the coaches at Ole Miss had asked me to drive up to Oxford so he could give me a campus tour and introduce me to professors, and when my dad asked what kind of professors, I said "History," thinking that would please him, which it didn't. The only thing that made sense to him, if nothing would do me but to attend college, was a business degree. I told him my former offensive line coach had asked me to hold some special one-on-one sessions with incoming varsity linemen, to work with them on various techniques like cross-blocks and cut-offs. I adhered to what I still think of as *Three Commandments for Liars*: one, provide a decent amount of detail but not too much, or it will be apparent that you're trying too hard; two, be consistent but not too consistent, or your account will lose the randomness of lived experience; three, and most importantly, if no information is demanded, don't provide any.

Most days nobody asked where I'd been. I was, of course, at the library. I usually got there about ten after three, just as fast as I could drive my old car across town. Unless it was raining, I didn't go inside, parking out back and waiting until she came out. There was a picnic table under a magnolia tree where we could sit and not been seen from the street. We were visible through the bathroom window, though, and it wouldn't be long before Miss LuAnn happened to look out.

It's easy to view all of this in the darkest possible terms, especially, if like me, you have spent much of your life teaching younger people and understand just how little ingenuity would be required to put the most fragile and insecure among them to whatever use you choose. All you have to do is win their trust. Generally speaking, that simply means paying them attention, behaving as if their thoughts and concerns, not to mention their hopes and dreams, are worthy of your consideration. I'm not going to say that there was never a time I hated her—because before too long, there surely would be and it would linger, off and on, until I met my wife—but today I recall her with fondness and no small measure of gratitude. I loved most of the time I spent with her, though those early days when we sat at the picnic table and did nothing but talk were the best.

Initially, we talked about books. In retrospect, nearly everything she read was relentlessly middlebrow. McCullers notwithstanding, her favorites seemed to be bestselling writers like Taylor Caldwell, James Michener, and Irving

Wallace. She thought *Jonathan Livingston Seagull* was a great book and urged me to read it. She said Irwin Shaw could be tedious or even downright difficult, but she thought I might like *The Young Lions*. Hemingway, she said, could be fun as long as you enjoyed fishing and bullfighting, but she wasn't drawn to either one. Faulkner was too overwrought for her taste. She'd read him, though, because this was Mississippi and you more or less had to. When I got ready to give it a go, I ought to start with *The Unvanquished*. At least in that one, he didn't throw up a wall of words to keep you out.

I asked her what Mr. Simmons liked to read, and she said, "Pete has never read a book in his life."

"Not even in college?"

She shrugged. "He was a business major. He made a C minus in freshman English, and the only reason he passed was that we were already dating and I wrote his research paper. He was assigned T.S. Eliot's play *The Cocktail Party*. It would've killed him to read it. To be honest, it nearly killed me."

She asked me plenty of questions about myself. Somehow, I overcame my inclination to lie. I'd already learned that neither Ole Miss nor Mississippi State planned to sign me because I was too small and didn't have the bone structure to add weight without becoming fat. Though I found this humiliating and hadn't told anybody else that I probably wouldn't get a Division 1 offer, I confessed it to her the first or second time we talked. I might end up, I said, someplace like Delta State.

"There's nothing wrong with that," she said.

"It's a podunk college."

"Well, we live in a podunk place." She asked what I intended to major in.

"English. Or maybe history."

"Do you plan to teach and coach?"

"No, ma'am. I plan to be a writer."

She didn't laugh, though it must have sounded delusional since my only identifiable qualification was that, like most of the people walking the streets of my hometown, I could string together several complete sentences. "Good for you," she said. "Most people don't know what they want to be when they're your age."

"Did you?"

"No, I did not."

Even when it began to grow colder, she would appear there, sometimes with a cup of coffee, sometimes not. I asked the kinds of questions that seemed safe, learning that she'd grown up on a farm, that her father owned a decent amount of good land up in Quitman County, that he'd died a few years earlier and her mother now lived with her sister in Fairhope, Alabama. She was in high school when rock 'n roll started, but she never really liked it. She loved Glen Miller, Tommy Dorsey, Benny Goodman and Tony Bennett. She said she was an awful cook.

An alley ran behind the building, bordered on both sides by people's back yards, with tall fences and hedgerows for most, though not all, of its block-long length. Some days we walked it two or three times, and once I saw a woman whose face I knew but whose name escaped me looking out the window at us. Unbeknownst to me, Miss LuAnn had already begun to talk. Jane would tell me later that she saw no change in her behavior, though given what I know about the effects of moral outrage, it seems to me unlikely that her colleague continued to treat her exactly like she had before these daily encounters occurred.

What, one might wonder, could have been going through my older friend's mind? She was as mainstream as they come. Each day she dressed properly. She baked cookies for her daughter's Brownie troop. She attended Bible study and sang in the choir. She voted Republican. Her husband was a member of the Chamber of Commerce and the Rotary Club, and a couple of years earlier they'd built a new house in the best part of town. She drove a new Lincoln Continental. She had a lot to lose.

One day, while we were walking, she suddenly said, "You don't have a girlfriend, do you?"

"No, ma'am." I mentioned the name of someone I'd had a couple of dates with. "We went to movies a few times, but that was about it."

"I don't know why you wouldn't have somebody," she said. "If I were a high school girl, I'd never let you out of my sight."

We kept walking. The day was cold and damp, but she wasn't wearing gloves and neither was I, and I wondered what would happen if I reached down and took her hand in mine. I kept thinking about it, trying to work up the nerve, all the while feeling the same trepidation I would have if I had decided to rob Planters Bank.

Before long, we got back to the library, and the two of us turned to face each other. "Well," she said, "I'll go ahead and wish you Happy Thanksgiving. I'm taking all of next week off."

Her lips were thin, and she either was not wearing lipstick or had chosen a shade so pale that you couldn't tell it was there. "Could I. . . ."

"Could you what?"

I faltered. I knew what I wanted to ask, but the words would not come out, and I was too innocent, or perhaps I should say too ignorant, to understand that words were not called for.

"Maybe one day," she said, then told me to enjoy the holiday and went back inside.

•

On the Monday after Thanksgiving, she never appeared. Waiting for her at the picnic table, I finally noticed that her Lincoln was not in the parking lot, but she sometimes walked to work, as they lived only about three blocks away. So I stepped into the library, thinking maybe she'd been delayed. No one was in there except Miss LuAnn and two or three book-browsers. The librarian gave me a strange look, her eyebrows knitting themselves together, her jaw setting grimly. I hung around a while longer, thinking maybe Mrs. Simmons would emerge from the bathroom, but that didn't happen. Eventually, I left.

I don't recall a whole lot about the next hour or so. I probably drove around town, or maybe I drove on out beyond the city limit sign, on the gravel farm roads. It seems to me that it was yet another gray, damp day—there were a lot of those that fall—and few sights are as bleak as a cotton field after scrap picking. There's nothing left but a bunch of broken stalks that whistle in the wind. If that's what I did, it could have only further darkened my mood. Something was wrong. I'll never know how I knew it, but I did.

Eventually, I stopped at a convenience store and bought a soft drink to break a dollar. Then I drove to a rundown motel on the edge of town, got out and walked over to the phone booth that stood underneath the neon sign that seldom, if ever, said *No Vacancy*. My heart was pounding, and it does not stretch the imagination to think that my hand shook as I fed the phone a dime and began to dial a number that I knew by heart though I had never placed a call to it before.

I would have hung up if her husband or her daughter answered, but the voice that said hello was hers.

"Hi," I said, "it's Steve."

"I knew it would be," she said. "Or anyway, I hoped it would be."

"Are you sick?"

"No. Just upset. Hold on. Let me close the door."

Her mother-in-law always picked their daughter up and kept her at their place until Jane got off work, so I thought maybe the little girl was sick and had to stay home. That turned out not to be true. She was at home for a different reason.

When she came back on the line, Mrs. Simmons told me that over the Thanksgiving break, her husband had told her he wanted her to quit her job, that he thought it was a bad idea for their daughter to spend the afternoons with her grandparents. This didn't make a lot of sense to her. He all but worshipped his parents, and so did their daughter. When she pressed him, he finally admitted that he'd heard about her afternoon "meetings" with me. She asked who he'd heard this from, and he turned red and said, "Multiple sources." She lost her temper then. They had a heated argument that led each of them to accuse the other of neglect. He said she wasn't meeting his needs, that she was cold, and she in turn brought up "the girl on the softball team."

I said, "What girl on the softball team?"

"Oh," she said, "you didn't hear about that. I just assumed you knew." So she filled me in, telling me how she had to wait a couple of weeks to find out whether he intended to leave her, how one day he came back from yet another session with the pastor and announced that he was staying, that even if they couldn't love each other passionately, they could love each other with *Agape.*

"With *what?*" I said.

"*Agape.* It's a Greek word. It means God's love. Our

minister conducts a small study group for people who want to know what the New Testament says in the original Greek. Pete goes to it, though I quit." She was silent for a moment, during which I took stock of my surroundings, realizing that everybody driving by on the highway could see me standing there having this conversation with a married woman. Though they would not know who I was talking to, the sense of danger I felt was exhilarating. "I've told you," she said, "a lot more than you probably expected to hear when you called."

She had, and I was aware that a barrier had been breached. Which of us had done the most to maintain it, I didn't know and still don't. I was just glad it had shattered. More than forty years later, I still feel that way. "Did you agree to quit your job?" I asked.

"He quoted *1st Peter*, *Ephesians* and *Colossians* to me— the necessity for wives to submit and obey. I didn't have much choice. That's how we live."

"Do you believe in all of that?"

"It's inconvenient. But I'm afraid I do."

It seemed incumbent upon me to make something happen, if anything was going to. I have placed myself in this situation more than once, and trying to think of a suitable metaphor that would capture the essence of such moments while skirting cliché seems pointless. So here are a few facts. A woman I spent some fruitfully fraught time with in graduate school was engaged to another man. The woman who helped me get past her when she married him was living with someone else at the time. My wife of thirty years, who came to the US from Poland on an academic exchange program, was married to someone else when I met her. My history is not spotty. It's badly stained. "I want to come over," I said.

"Over where?"

"To your house."

She did not ask if I'd lost my mind. It went without saying that to varying degrees both of us had and that unless she said no, we were going to court the kind of trouble that can lead to one of those crimes of passion you occasionally read about in small-town newspapers, where decorum forces the suppression of certain facts that would allow the reader to draw the correct conclusions about motives. Often, the readers of those newspapers have already drawn the correct conclusions. By the time the crime occurs, they've been predicting it for months. Everybody could see it coming but the victims, and sometimes they can see it coming too but lack the critical faculties to prevent it. Sometimes they plain don't care.

"Not today," she said. "He'll be back before long."

"What about tomorrow afternoon?"

"Afternoons aren't good. From now on I'll have my daughter." She could have stopped right there, and if she had, it's likely, I believe, that I would have stopped too. Off the football field, I'd never been tenacious. Acceptance of defeat was in my DNA.

"Wednesday morning," she said, "he's going to a meeting

with the insurance commissioner down in Jackson."

I would need to cut school. But I had cut school before. "What time?" I asked.

Over the noise of the cars and trucks passing on the highway, I heard her sigh. "Around ten," she said, then requested that I park at least a couple of blocks away.

•

The car I drove was a 1963 green Ford Galaxie. Two years earlier, my father had bought it for next to nothing so that I could drive myself to town and back. If it sounds extravagant for someone in his financial condition to buy his son a car, it wasn't: for one thing, the private school had no bus routes in our part of the county; and for another, the Galaxy was falling apart. Hit hard from behind before we acquired it, it had no rear bumper, the trunk lid had been replaced with one from a maroon-colored model and never repainted, and one rear quarter panel was so badly rusted you could shove your hand through it. In the black part of town, it might have blended in. On our side, it stood out. Everybody knew who drove it.

So like a spy practicing sound tradecraft, I parked it downtown, in the lot behind the Piggly Wiggly. Her house was about eight blocks away, and to get there I had to walk past the bank, the fire station, the police station, two or three churches and about thirty homes. That I was doing this on a weekday morning and that I was easily recognizable in my letter jacket, with my number on one arm and my All-Conference patch on the other, did not give me pause.

I had no idea what Mrs. Simmons—for that was how I still thought of her—planned to do with me. All we'd ever done was talk, and we'd never talked about sex. For all I knew, I might be attending a two-member book club. If anything, this made me even more nervous than I might have been if I'd felt sure that when she opened the door, she'd be standing there in a sheer negligee. The only women I'd been behind closed doors with were blood relatives: my mother, my grandmother, my aunts.

By the time I reached her block, I was terrified. I would not have been this scared if you'd told me I had to cover a kickoff against the Dallas Cowboys. If cell phones had existed, I would have called her number and reported that I was sick. But they didn't, so I plodded on down the block, walked up to her door and knocked. The final few seconds in which I might have spared all of us—my mother and father, her husband and daughter, and certainly myself—the misery that was to follow slipped away. If I don't include her on that list, it's because I have always been convinced that if it hadn't been me at her door, sooner or later it would have been someone else. She would have worked at the library until it happened. I was not the only bookish boy in town. She hadn't taken a lot of risks in her life. She was determined to take one now.

She did not open the door in a negligee. She was again wearing the beige dress, though this time there was a dark brown sash around her waist, which either hadn't been there before or else had escaped my notice. She had on those sensible shoes. I know because the instant the door swung open, and I saw her standing there, I dropped my gaze, so that I was literally staring at the floor.

She did not say a word: not *Hello*, not *Good morning*, not *Hurry up and come in*. Nothing. She just stepped to the side to let me enter, and because there seemed to be no other option, I did.

I have no idea if my recollections of the house's interior are accurate or not. What I recall is white tile in the foyer, a gold-plated chandelier, an absurdly oversized oval mirror in which I could see all of my body except my feet and an inch or two of each shin. She turned and led me into the living room, where the heavy green drapes remained closed. Shag carpeting that matched the drapes, a small fireplace that looked like no fire had ever been built there, gold-plated andirons. Matching couch, loveseat and armchair, all of them overstuffed and covered in gray fabric speckled with tiny pink roses. On the glass-topped coffee table, several issues of *Life*. According to what I just learned online, that magazine had ceased publication back in 1972, so either I'm wrong or they were old copies. Nevertheless, we will leave them right there, where they have lain for forty-two years.

"Can I get you something to drink?" she asked. "There are some Cokes in the refrigerator, and I think maybe a

Mountain Dew or a 7Up. Or I could make you a cup of coffee."

I asked for the Coke. Someone, somewhere, had told me that Coke could settle your stomach, and mine needed settling. I have not mentioned this until now, because it's something I seldom think about anymore, but I always threw up before football games. It's not that uncommon, as anybody who has seriously played the sport will tell you. The butterflies always passed as soon as I hit somebody, but there was no one to hit now and there wouldn't be unless her husband suddenly showed up. As odd as it may sound, I had not considered that possibility until I sat down on the couch. What if he'd forgotten something and had to turn around and come back? What if he'd made the trip up, just to see if he could catch her fooling around? I didn't know that day that he had a gun, but since most men in the Delta owned not just one but quite a few, the possibility should have occurred to me sooner. There wasn't a whole lot somebody his size could do to somebody my size except shoot him.

I took the canned Coke. As I popped the tab, my hand shook.

She'd sat down on the loveseat, which was adjacent to the sofa. "You're nervous," she said. "Are you sure you want to be here?"

"Yes ma'am."

"Then I think maybe you should stop saying 'yes ma'am.'

I don't believe this is a 'yes ma'am' kind of situation. I don't think honorifics are called for either."

I didn't know what the word "honorific" meant. I thought it had something to do with official titles: Queen Elizabeth, President Ford.

My confusion must have been obvious. "I mean I don't want you to keep calling me Mrs. Simmons," she said. "I think if you call me that again, Steve, I'm either going to scream or cry. I don't know which. Maybe both."

I could not imagine her crying, and I couldn't imagine her screaming, though I often felt the impulse to do both myself: not that long ago, on the day I learned that neither Ole Miss nor Mississippi State planned to offer me a scholarship, I'd gone down to the drainage ditch that sometimes flooded our house and howled for five or ten minutes. The other thing I could not imagine, though I had often tried, was what she would be like when she made love. She seemed so cool, so placid, that it was hard to think of her giving in to physical urges or losing control of her emotions. My assumptions about her were not that far off the mark. It would be a while longer before I found that out. But once I did, it would color every relationship I had until ten years later, when I stepped into a room at a university in Virginia and met the woman who became my wife.

I don't know how long we sat there before we said another word. Probably no more than a couple of minutes, though it felt like an hour. Finally I said, "So from now on, you're Jane."

Her smile looked forced. It had not occurred to me to wonder if she was scared herself. Something else that had not occurred to me was that she might want her husband to return and find us there. I wouldn't think of that until some months later. But for a long time—the mostly miserable haze that my early and mid-twenties would turn into—I accepted it as the absolute truth that I was little more than a pawn, a toy for an unhappy older woman to play with. To think like that, of course, reduces a complex mix of human emotions to the status of a tweet.

"In practical terms," she said, "'from now on' simply means until you leave for college. After that, I'll be neither Jane nor Mrs. Simmons. From your perspective, I will quickly become nobody at all."

All the relationships I ever had with women started tentatively, with plenty of reticence and reserve on my part. And all of them have turned, for better or worse, on a single moment of boldness that, when I consider it later, will surprise and, occasionally, chill me.

I considered telling her she was wrong, that she would always remain at the center of my life, but I didn't do that until much later, when my profession of undying affection was the last thing she wanted to hear. I also considered rising off the couch, stepping over the loveseat, sitting down, pulling her close and kissing her. Instead, I posed a question: "Are you in love with me?" The words horrified me as soon as they'd left my mouth. I sat there in stunned silence.

She had a string in her hands, a piece of twine maybe four inches long. I don't know where it came from, or why she had it, but I have never forgotten it. She held one end of it between her left thumb and index finger while twisting the other end around the index finger on her right hand. She twisted it, pulled her finger free, then twisted it tight again. She did that two or three times, looking past me at the fireplace.

"Yes," she finally said. "I'm afraid that I am."

•

Winter in the Mississippi Delta is worse than people in other parts of the country might suspect. The forests were long ago cut down so the land could be farmed. Trees are few and far between, especially in the countryside. From the first of December through sometime in mid- to late-March, when the barren fields are disked to prepare them for spring planting, there is almost nothing to break the wind. When it comes screaming down off the Great Plains, it gets a good crack at you. If you live in a house like the one we lived in, with only space heaters, the rooms are often cold and drafty. Even worse is what you see when you step outside: brownish-gray mud that extends to infinity. I'd always experienced a sinking sensation after the first of the year, when it felt like there wasn't much to look forward to.

Having accepted a scholarship to play for a Division II school twenty-five miles from home, I should have been preparing myself for the following season by lifting weights, running sprints and doing agility drills. Instead, I spent all my attention on the kind of romantic relationship that could plausibly exist in the Victorian era between people who felt affection for each other but were not married. Rather than taking the epistolary form, though, our relationship depended on the telecommunications system.

For a while—since on weekday afternoons I was often home alone—I spoke to her from our phone. The problem was that we were on that feature of mid-century rural American life known as the party-line. Nine other families shared it with us, so during the course of nearly every call, you would hear one or two people pick up to dial a number. Most of them, being well-mannered folks, hung up the second they heard voices, but one or two did not. I strongly suspected that an old man who lived on the other side of the drainage ditch and was known as Mr. Cy, short for Cyrus, was a frequent listener, and unfortunately his house and truck were insured by Jane's husband. After a couple of weeks, she requested that I quit calling from home and use public phones.

Before long, I knew where every pay phone in the county was located. For obvious reasons, I preferred those in out-of-the-way places. My absolute favorite was attached to a pole behind the Piggly Wiggly, on the banks of the bayou that bisected our town. Why anybody would think it appropriate to place a phone where virtually nobody would ever look for one was a mystery, but I have always been thankful that somebody did. Unfortunately, that phone was frequently out-of-order, so it was not dependable. Another one that I often used was, ironically, in front of the telephone company. The building was only two blocks from Jane's house, and it wouldn't have been smart to use it on weekdays, when people stopped by to pay bills or request maintenance. But it stood on a quiet street, and its proximity to the Simmons' home solved a problem: if I drove by their house on Saturday or Sunday and saw Pete Simmons' car gone, I could place a call within no more than sixty seconds.

On my visit to her house—one of only two times I ever stepped inside it—we hadn't done anything but talk, because the longer we sat there, the more nervous both of us became about the prospect of his returning unannounced. I didn't even kiss her before leaving. But the content of that conversation changed everything, beginning with the character of all the conversations we conducted over the phone in the next few months, not to mention what happened when we finally ended up together in her car, in somebody's cotton field late one night.

The talk had turned overtly sexual, and in that respect it became a kind of foreplay, which was curiously sanitized, even clinical. Body parts, when she referred to them, went by their legal names: breast, penis, buttocks. "Fucking" was "intercourse" and what the man did to begin it was "en-tuh" the woman. I adopted her vocabulary, found it magnificently stimulating and seldom left a pay phone un-aroused. I came to view the phones themselves as objects of affection.

She told me sex never had been that good for her. Something just wasn't right. Over time she revealed what the "something wrong" was: she clung to the notion that the only "real" orgasm came during vaginal intercourse, and so far she'd apparently never experienced one of those. She said she believed it would be different when she was with me, and I hastened to assure her it would, though I didn't have a clue what she was talking about. Didn't everybody come when they fucked?

We talked of the day when we could be married. If this sounds far-fetched, even insane, I should mention that the following year, after I'd already gone to college, a teacher at my school got involved with one of her students and left her husband for him. She was about twice his age, too. They moved to another town, and my recollection is that they stayed together for many years. For Jane and me, though, this future was a decade away: she told me she couldn't leave Mr. Simmons until her daughter finished school. She said she wouldn't blame me if I chose not to wait that long. But she made it clear that if I started dating girls in college, things would be over between us. She'd been badly disappointed in her marriage. She refused to be disappointed again.

I responded with perhaps the only non-mawkishly sentimental line that left my mouth during any of these overheated conversations: "Hell, I've already waited eighteen years," I stoically replied. "I can stand ten more."

I meant what I said. I believed I could weather whatever

I had to, any kind of pain, loneliness or deprivation, for however long it lasted, if she was the glittering prize that awaited me when my trials were over. That I was in the grips of a fevered obsession is obvious That I was deluded io too. But perhaps due to the iron hand that ruled the house I'd grown up in, I had learned fairly early how to withdraw into my own imagination, where things worked out better than they did in real life. Here was a *grown woman*—that phrase kept going through my mind—who had a college degree, who'd read a lot of books, who'd traveled, who lived in a nice house and drove a nice car, and she was willing to give all that up for me, if I could only remain devoted until she was free.

·

Her husband, of course, found out. How could he have failed to? One day, in late afternoon, he called the house off and on for nearly two hours, but the phone was constantly busy. He must have already had his suspicions because, rather than ask if she'd taken the phone off the hook to get a little nap, he said nothing. He tried again the next day and got the same busy signal. He got a busy signal the following Saturday when he went to the country club to play golf. He got a busy signal again and again and again. He asked his daughter what Mom did in the afternoons, and she said her mom was always in the bedroom, with the door closed, talking on the phone. A couple of times, when she picked up the phone in the living room, she heard the other person's voice. Was it another woman's voice? he asked, at a cost I can only imagine. Or did the other voice belong to a man? A man, his daughter said.

Before I go any further, I need to reveal this: ten years ago, when I was fifty, I ran into a seventy-two-year-old Pete Simmons in the Memphis airport. I was with my eighteen-year-old daughter, who was buying a magazine for our flight back to California. Pete was with his second wife, whom he'd been married to for many years. They had just entered the Hudson News shop, and there was no way to get out of there without walking past them. When we made eye contact, it was clear that he recognized me. I'd heard he moved to Memphis back in the late eighties, but I'd forgotten.

I hoped he'd ignore me, but instead he took his wife's hand and together they approached the checkout stand. To my surprise, a broad smile appeared on his face.

He told me hello, and we shook hands, and he said how glad he was to see me, then introduced me to his wife and I introduced them both to my daughter.

"Honey," Pete said to her, "I'm sure you know your dad's a fine writer. But I'll tell you something you may not know. He was also one of the greatest football players our hometown ever produced. It's a shame you didn't get to watch him play. Lord, he gave opposing quarterbacks fits. I never saw anything quite like it." We talked a few more minutes, then headed off to catch our flight, and I assume they went off to catch theirs. That was the last time I ever saw him—the only time I've seen him in forty years.

I mention this encounter because, when I was eighteen years old—the same age as my daughter was that day in the airport—I wreaked havoc on this man's life and that of his own daughter. Until that day in Memphis, he had remained frozen in my mind, the same forty-year-old man who chased me all over town one night, his headlights no more than a foot or two from my rear bumper. Fearing he might shoot me, I finally wheeled into the parking lot outside the police station, thinking that at least if he did it there, they could quickly summon medical help.

I will remain grateful to the end of my days for the little coda those few minutes in the airport provided. On our flight to California, I thought I finally understood why Larry McMurtry had returned to the characters in *The Last Picture Show*, with the sequels *Texasville* (1987) and *Duane's Depressed* (2003). I hadn't liked *Texasville*, which seemed strained to me, and I resisted the inclination to read *Duane's Depressed*, just as I have resisted *When the Light Goes* and *Rhino Ranch*, the two sequels that followed in 2008 and 2009. Reviewers and interviewers have speculated for years that Sonny Crawford's friend Duane, who is at the center of all the sequels, is McMurtry's alter ego. Whether that's true or not, I understand the hold those characters clearly exercise over the author.

At a certain point, I think, it's natural to want one more conversation with those whose lives intersected yours when you were young and, to whatever degree, helped shape the adult you've become. The chance meeting with Pete Simmons, and the generosity he showed my daughter and me, felt like an ending of sorts, and I view it with nothing but gratitude.

In the spring of 1975, though, I hated him as I had never hated anyone before and have never hated anyone since. I thought him the worst kind of religious hypocrite, a man who'd lost his head over a girl himself, then reacted with outrage when he found out his wife had done something similar. He'd gotten what he deserved, I thought, and here he was trying to keep me from getting what I deserved. And, after all, I had so little. Even my football stardom had been taken away when the big schools passed me over.

One day he phoned our house. It was a Saturday, and my mother was at work, my father pulling a weekend shift at the TV transmitter. Mr. Simmons told me who was calling, then said he'd confronted his wife, and she had admitted I was the one she'd been talking to and claimed she'd fallen in love with me. He sounded strangely calm and, before I could respond, he asked if I could possibly come by their house to talk things over.

At the time, I could not understand why he didn't ask to speak to my father and tell him, in the strongest possible terms, to keep me from calling his wife. It never occurred to me that he was treating me like another man, rather than a horny teenager. Nor did it occur to me how embarrassing it would be for him if the word got out around town that his wife had lost her head over a high school football player. The third thing beyond my ken was the fear he must have felt for his daughter and the effect all of this might have on her.

I've always had a soft voice, which has never quite seemed to belong with my body. That afternoon, I tried to make it sound deep and resonant. "Sure," I said, as though I were granting him a huge favor, "I'll be happy to come over and talk."

When I arrived, he opened the door. I could claim to recall exactly how he was dressed, but I don't, except that I know he wore a green sleeveless V-necked vest. He said, "Mrs. Simmons is waiting for us back in the bedroom." He stood there for a moment, and it only occurred to me later that he was waiting to see if I would proceed to that destination on my own. Since I'd never been to the bedroom, all I could do was wait for him to lead the way. Eventually, he did but not until asking me if I'd like something to drink, which I politely declined.

I have urged countless young fiction writers to ask themselves why they are setting their scenes in one place instead of another. If three characters take part, is one of them hindered by the setting, like a football team playing a road game? My guess is that by conducting our conversation in his and his wife's bedroom, Pete Simmons intended to secure home field advantage. It was not a bad choice. When he opened the door and stood aside, there sat Jane on a tiny sofa adjacent to the bed. Though I probably didn't know the term "Rococo"—or, if I did, was clueless as to its meaning—I believe it could have been applied to that piece of furniture: I recall an elaborately carved, asymmetrical backrest, and I believe the upholstery had an acanthus leaf motif, though I definitely did not know the word "acanthus" at the time. The sofa seemed to have been designed with my discomfort in mind, and unfortunately there was nowhere else in the room to sit. When Mr. Simmons gestured at it, I had no option but to take a seat beside his wife.

"Steve," he said, "as I told you on the phone, this morning Mrs. Simmons informed me that she believes she's in love with you. I told her that there's a difference in love and infatuation, and that what she's experiencing is the latter. I suspect that what you're experiencing is simple lust. It's a normal enough thing for young men to feel, so I'm not judging you for that. The purpose of this conversation is for you and Mrs. Simmons to understand that even leaving morality aside, these are temporary emotions. I think she has come to understand that over the last few hours, and I hope that you'll assure me now that you do too. Then we won't have to take this any further."

I am not sure what I would have said if I had been the first to respond. I suspect I would have puffed myself up and told him that I knew the difference between love and infatuation, which I did not, and between love and lust, though I did not understand that distinction either. What I understood was what I wanted right then, that minute. Nothing else mattered. In other words, he was one hundred percent correct. I was not thinking beyond the moment.

Jane spoke before I could formulate a reply. "That's absolutely not what I understand," she said.

The effect her statement had on Pete Simmons is difficult to describe, though I remember it as if it had happened thirty seconds ago. His face did not change color, his body language betrayed nothing, he continued to stand there near the foot of their bed with his arms crossed over that green sleeveless vest. But I could see something different in his eyes, and I believed I had seen it before, on the football field, that it was the same thing you saw in the eyes of your opponent when he realized he was beaten. There was an element of panic involved, but it usually took a back seat to disbelief. It was a sight I had always relished, and I am sorry to admit that I did that day as well. What I did not grasp, though I would soon be forced to, was that nobody thought we were involved in a contest except me.

"You understood it," Mr. Simmons said, "before *he* showed up."

"Then maybe you shouldn't have asked him to *show* up. Anyway, what I said I understood was the difference between love and commitment. You can have the latter without the former. I told you I was committed to you until Susan graduates from high school. If you'd listened, you would have understood that. And then maybe you wouldn't have picked the phone up and called him. I asked you not to. But you never hear me. You never have. You just quote the Bible."

He was angry then—there was no mistaking it. His face hardened, as if a coat of lacquer had been applied. He stared at her for a moment, then looked at me. "You can have her," he said, then turned and left the room, pulling the door shut behind him.

So there we sat, his wife and me. For the first time, we touched, as she took one of my hands in both of hers and leaned against me. I caught a whiff of fragrance. The few girls I'd messed around with hadn't smelled like her. They usually smelled like beer.

"I don't think he means it," she said. "He'll be back. Probably in no time."

She was right: in no more than a minute or two, we heard heavy footsteps. She let go of my hand and leaned away from me just a second before the door opened. He didn't enter, just said, "Steve, I think it's time for you to go now." He turned and disappeared, and I whispered, "What's next?"

"It won't be easy," she said, "but my feelings haven't changed." She said to call her on Monday afternoon but hang up unless she was the one who answered.

As I left, I saw him standing in the living room, his back to the hallway. Though he must have heard me, he never turned around to watch me go. I thought I saw his shoulders shaking, but that didn't bother me any more than watching a running back I'd tackled limp off the field. My view of the world was very simple: there were winners, and there were losers, and it was Pete Simmons' turn to join the second group. I'd been a dues-paying member for most of my life.

•

When I called the following Monday afternoon, he answered, so I hung up. The same thing happened on Tuesday. Wednesday afternoon, I drove down their street. His car was parked alongside hers. The same was true the next day and the day after that and all through the weekend. He had basically placed her under house arrest.

The next afternoon when I drove by he was gone, so I hurried to the phone behind the Piggly Wiggly and dialed their number. I got a recording telling me it had been disconnected. I slammed the receiver against the post where the phone was mounted, cracking the device wide open, so that a couple of wires and the tiny speaker in the listening end dangled loosely.

The next day I skipped school, drove by their house around nine a.m. and saw that both their cars were gone. I drove past his office and saw his car parked out front. In a town the size of ours, there were relatively few places to go. Two grocery stores, three pharmacies, the clothing stores on Front Street, a couple of beauty salons, the dry cleaner's, the hardware, the Western Auto, the bank, the doctor's office, the hospital. I knew she didn't shop at Piggly Wiggly anymore, so I drove to its competitor, Sunflower Food

Store, which was out on the main highway. There stood her Lincoln, and there she happened to be, waiting by the door while the black man who sacked groceries placed her purchases in the trunk. I waited until he turned and began to push the cart toward the store. Then I jumped out of my car and reached her just as she was closing the door.

To say that she looked fearful would not do the moment justice. "This is dangerous," she said, her eyes scanning the highway, where cars and trucks were cruising past. "Follow me to the football field. But park on the visitors' side."

The advantage to parking on that side was immediately clear. The houses over there were little boxy rental properties, where working class white people came and went. We might be seen, but nobody who saw us was likely to matter all that much. Their kids, if they had any, probably belonged to the tiny white minority at the otherwise all-black public school.

She opened her door but didn't get out of her car, so I squatted down behind it on the side next to the stadium, where it would be hard for anybody to see who she was talking to. "He's threatening to take Susan away from me," she said, "unless we quit talking. I should've seen this coming. I don't know what I was thinking."

My voice, as I said earlier, has always been soft. Back then, if I raised it, it sometimes broke. I imagine that's what happened that day. "So what does this mean?" I said.

"It means," she said, "that we can't talk on the phone anymore."

I pleaded with her to give me their new number but to no avail. It would kill her, she said, if she lost her daughter. I didn't have children. When I did, I'd understand.

"So this," I finally said, standing and waving my hand around, in a gesture intended to encompass the football stadium and the dingy houses across the street and perhaps the rest of what suddenly seemed to me a miserable little town, with miserable little people whose influence I would never be free of, "this is how it fucking *ends*?"

"Please don't scream at me," she said. "But yes, I'm afraid this is how it ends." She reached up, grabbed my hand and squeezed it, then shut her door, started the car and drove away.

·

That was neither how, nor when, it ended.

It was instead the beginning of the darkest period of my life, a time when I suffered one self-inflicted wound after another, in the process causing a few hundred sleepless nights for both my parents, wrecking what remained of the Simmons' marriage, running up massive phone bills that my mother borrowed money from friends to pay off, ruining whatever chance I might have had to excel on the football field, getting myself placed on academic probation, winding up hospitalized because I couldn't sleep and had lost my appetite. I would eventually be prescribed Elavil, a tricyclic antidepressant that I quickly became dependent on and remained addicted to for several years. The damage I did to myself would only wear off a decade later, after I walked into a room in Blacksburg, Virginia, where an orientation for new Virginia Tech instructors was about to take place, and sat down beside a woman with shoulder-length black hair, a dark complexion, large eyes and—though I only learned this when we introduced ourselves—a Slavic accent. I will remain forever grateful that by then I knew enough about writers like Musil, Broch, Hrabal, Kundera, and Konwicki to initiate a conversation. Since that day I have led a mostly charmed life.

It was anything but charmed in 1975 and 1976. For a month or two I honored Jane's request and left her alone, though I often drove by and gazed at her house. I began to drink a good bit, and while I continued to lift weights, I did no real conditioning work and put on more pounds than I could carry. Many nights I went to bed drunk. On prom night, four of us who didn't have dates drove over to Greenville and were arrested outside a club by two white cops for talking to several black people. They charged all of us, black and white alike, with creating a disturbance. Because I wasn't quite as drunk as the other three, we pooled our resources to bail me out, and I called the father of one of the others, who came and paid our fines. Fortunately, the Greenville paper, the *Delta Democrat–Times*, was considered dangerously liberal and we didn't subscribe, so my dad never saw the arrest log.

I was every bit as lost as Sonny Crawford after the

deaths of Sam the Lion and Billy, the destruction of his friendship with Duane, the demise of his affair with Ruth Popper and the annulment of his marriage to Jacy Farrow. I had nowhere to go, nobody to talk to. My former friends no longer interested me, and I no longer interested them. Books couldn't hold my attention. I'd start one, read a few pages, realize I couldn't recall a word of it, then lay it down beside all the others I'd given up on. I tried to reread *The Last Picture Show* but couldn't get through the first chapter.

One day that summer, I had to drive up to the college I would be attending in the fall and complete some paperwork related to my football scholarship. Walking out of the administration building, I came face to face with Jane Simmons. Because we hadn't talked for a couple of months, I didn't know she'd decided to take a summer school class.

She was not unhappy to see me.

On November 8, 2016, Donald J. Trump won 88.7 percent of the vote in Archer County, Texas. Since he received only 52.6 percent of the vote statewide, it's fair to conclude that the citizens of Archer County might be significantly more conservative than a great many of those in what has traditionally been one of the most conservative states.

According to the latest census figures I've been able to find, the county's per capita income is $23,888, which places Archer in the top quarter of the state's 254 counties. It's ninety-four percent white, about what it was during the era in which *The Last Picture Show* is set. Sixty-two percent of the county's households self-identify as "married, living together." Ninety percent of the population self-identifies as heterosexual.

The population of Archer City itself is listed as 1,834. It's roughly eighty-three percent white and nine percent Hispanic. It has six churches, or one for every three hundred people in town. In my Mississippi hometown, which currently has a population of a little over ten thousand, there are forty-two churches, or roughly one for every 245 people. The national average for the US is about one church for every 900 people. In Boston, it's one for every 1100 people, and in San Antonio it's one for every 2460 people. I mention these figures because it would seem reasonable to conclude that both the town I hail from and the real-life model for Thalia are exceptionally godly places.

Yet on November 11, 2016, three days after the presidential election, the Archer City girls' volleyball team played a team from Fort Hancock, which is near the Texas/Mexico border. Ninety-seven percent of the students in the Fort Hancock school district are Hispanic. According to the Fort Worth *Star–Telegram*, during the game Archer City students repeatedly chanted "Build a Wall" at the opposing team and its supporters. Archer City school superintendent C. D. Knobloch apologized later, while noting that "our students are not racists. It's as simple as that." His Fort Hancock counterpart, Jose Franco, accepted the apology but said that "I guess what bothered me most was no adults, no officials did anything about it while the match was going on."

So much for loving thy neighbor, should thy neighbor's skin be darker than thine.

I know none of the people involved, and I am by no means suggesting that kids in Archer City are somehow worse than those in other towns around the country. But what I am suggesting is that kids often repeat what they've heard at home. It seems reasonable to think that Trump's promises to build a wall along the border with Mexico did not displease too many of the Archer City students' parents, especially since nearly ninety percent of them voted for him.

Archer City being fairly insular, it also seems likely that the high school kids chanting "Build a wall" are the grandchildren or perhaps great-grandchildren of people whom Larry McMurtry, now eighty years old, might have known in the fifties, when *The Last Picture Show* takes place. Based on what I know of towns like it, or like the one I grew up in, which, despite being a lot more diverse than Archer City, nevertheless has remained home to many of the same families since the mid-to-late nineteenth century, there's a lot of continuity from generation to generation. Many of the guys I grew up with and played football with have remained there in the town where they were born sixty years ago. Their opinions usually don't differ that much from their parents'. I'd be surprised if some of the same attitudes and concerns on display in McMurty's novel and the classic film it gave birth to have disappeared from the hearts and minds of those in Archer City.

•

Religious zeal and its frequent sidekick—hypocrisy—are personified in this novel by the minister Brother Blanton.

His son Joe Bob, a virgin at seventeen, is constantly being tormented by his own lust. Some years earlier, Brother Blanton "slipped into his room one night and caught him masturbating by flashlight over a picture of [film star] Esther Williams." The episode led to a severe whipping at the hands of his father, who also tells him that if he continues to do it, he will eventually end up in the state insane asylum. Brother Blanton conjures a hellish vision of what Joe Bob can expect to find upon arrival, warning that hundreds of pathetic creatures are confined there, all of them "rotting away," and that the vast majority destroyed their mental faculties by doing exactly what he caught Joe Bob doing.

My guess is that this was a common experience of boys designated by fate, chance or the Almighty—take your pick—for birth in the Bible Belt in the mid-twentieth century, and for all I know, it may be common there even now, in these supposedly more enlightened times. Like me, Joe Bob tries to stop but fails miserably.

As a high school junior, he becomes convinced that he has gotten the call to preach, but the call has more to do with sexual guilt than hearing a voice from on high. He believes that girls will like him if he becomes a preacher and that this will help him lead a decent life. But the night he preaches his initial sermon, he gives in to temptation, and in no time he concludes he was mistaken in believing he'd been called to preach. It's easy enough for him to quit thinking about the Lord, but the only way he can get girls off his mind is by "jacking off."

His ultimate undoing is brought on by the shaming of the high school English teacher, a man named John Cecil, and it has plenty to do with sex and guilt. Mr. Cecil is married to "a fat bossy woman" and has two daughters. Sonny and Duane and some of their friends have occasionally wondered if he might be gay, for the simple reason that in the summertime he often drives groups of boys over to the irrigation ditch to go for a swim. He never joins them, just sits on the bank and watches them having their fun. Nobody seems to have a problem with this. Everyone likes Mr. Cecil.

The trouble starts when he talks the star football player Bobby Logan into taking a summer school class at the high school in nearby Wichita Falls. The teacher is taking a summer school class at the college in that city, so he gives Bobby a ride each day. This arouses the suspicions of Coach Popper, who the reader already knows fancies Bobby himself. The coach mentions his suspicions to a group of men at the filling station, noting that if there is anything he hates, "'it's to see a goddamn homasexyul messing around with a bunch of young kids.'" The other men are instantly moved to action because, as one of them says, teaching English is a woman's job anyway. Within twenty-four hours, on the basis of no evidence whatsoever of any wrongdoing, John Cecil is called before the school board and fired. The board members don't even question Bobby Logan, to see if Mr. Cecil has laid a hand on him, "because his father didn't want him to know what homosexuality was yet. If it had already happened to him, his father preferred that he didn't realize it."

In the aftermath of this scandal, "the church ladies," as McMurtry calls them, decide it's time for "an All City Revival." Rather than waste money on a traveling evangelist, they decide to call on the six local preachers, plus a few retirees and Joe Bob, who will be required to preach two sermons. The young man is presently beset by a spiritual crisis: "During the winter his ministerial flame had burned very low—he was not even confident that he himself was saved. He knew that he harbored hatred in his heart for about three-quarters of the boys of the town, and that was surely not a Christian attitude." Though uninspired, he makes it through the first of his two sermons without mishap. The second, however, will be on Saturday night, the evening before the revival is supposed to conclude, and it poses a terrible dilemma, due to his awareness that on the penultimate night of a revival, failure to win a good many rededications of faith will lead to disgrace.

Saturday arrives, and the day is hellishly hot. Brooding in his room, he masturbates a couple of times, then jumps in the car and drives around for a little while out beyond the city limits. When he gets back to town, he lures a little girl named Molly Clarg into his car by promising her a lemon sucker. There are witnesses to the abduction, and word travels fast.

Informed of the kidnapping, the sheriff mounts a search, finding Joe Bob parked with Molly on a lovers' lane just outside town. Her panties are lying on the back seat. Though a doctor's examination reveals that Molly has not been raped, Joe Bob is nevertheless arrested, leading to several nights in the local jail but releasing him from the more onerous fate of having to preach a sermon. Instead, his father occupies the pulpit that evening and delivers a fervent denunciation of his own son, telling the crowd that he has asked God to send Joe Bob to prison, because there are times when "'things just don't work out, and I believe it is God's merciful will that Joe Bob go to suffer with the murderer and the thief.'" The response is overwhelming, as nearly everybody in town flocks to the alter, "weeping and hugging one another, the women all slapping at their faces with damp powder puffs, trying to keep their makeup from running completely off."

The one exception is Lois Farrow. Upon hearing the minister call for his son to go to prison, she walks out of the revival, heads down to the jail and makes the deputy let her play checkers with Joe Bob, who beats her two games out of three. There's plenty of faith on display in Thalia, but the only one who seems capable of showing Joe Bob any Christian charity is Lois.

Another person who is shown virtually no charity is Ruth Popper. After Sonny drops her unceremoniously so that he can spend his time with the much younger and more appealing Jacy Farrow, Ruth falls into despair, rarely leaving the house. No one, she thinks, will ever desire her again or even want to know her.

All of the women in the neighborhood take to paying her unwanted visits, obviously eager to rub her loss in a little more deeply. Her treatment at their hands, and at the hands of Jacy, who delights when she runs into her at the grocery store—where the younger woman flashes her a huge smile and says, "Haven't seen you in a long time. I thought you must have left town for the summer'"—represent small-town malice at its worst.

•

It's this absence of empathy that Sam the Lion addresses following an episode in which Duane, Sonny and a few other boys arrange for Billy to have sex with the local prostitute.

Billy is a tragic figure from the moment he first appears in the novel until the day he is run over by a cattle truck as he obliviously sweeps the street on a windy morning. Born to a developmentally disabled mother who died while giving birth, he has been abandoned by his father and taken in by Sam the Lion, who acts as his protector.

The prostitute the boys fix him up with over Sonny's mild objections is an enormous woman named Jimmie Sue, a local carhop who turns tricks on the side. In addition to being physically grotesque and always smelling like onions, she's a racist, fond of saying that for the right price she'll have sex with anybody except "'Mixicans and niggers.'" She tries to bargain with the boys, pointing out that since Billy is an adolescent, not to mention "'an idiot,'" she ought to get two dollars rather than the dollar and a half she initially agreed on, but they won't budge, so she eventually gives in.

While she waits in the cab of the pickup, the boys throw Billy down on the ground and pull off everything but his shirt. He hasn't the faintest idea what's about to happen. They pick him up and shove him into the cab with Jimmy Sue, who is sprawled across the seat with her legs spread. The problem is that even though Billy achieves an erection, he doesn't know what to do with it and ends up ejaculating on the carhop's stomach. Jimmy Sue erupts, punching him and bloodying his nose.

When the boys get back to the poolhall with him, there's blood all over his shirt. He races inside, leaving them to face Sam, who, we've been told in the novel's opening pages, "took care of things, particularly boys." No stranger to suffering, he lost all three of his sons to various accidents, and eventually his wife went mad. Sam owns the three properties that, taken together, form the town's social nexus: the picture show, the all-night café, the poolhall. He in turn represents the town's moral center, and when he learns what the boys have done to Billy, he reacts accordingly:

"Boys, get on home," he said. "I'm done with all of you. I don't want to associate with you anymore and I don't want Billy to, either. Scaring an unfortunate creature like Billy when there ain't no reason to scare him is just plain trashy behavior. I've seen a lifetime of it and I'm tired of putting up with it. You can just stay out of this poolhall and out of my picture show and café too."

One can easily imagine him expressing the same weary disgust for the Archer City students who, in a state of euphoria following the election of a candidate promising to make America great again and labeling Mexicans as rapists, repeatedly shouted "Build a Wall" at the volleyball team from Fort Hancock.

If my town had a man like Sam the Lion, I'm sorry to say, I did not have the good fortune to run across him while growing up.

In 2003, when we were still living in California, my wife Ewa and I and our daughters Antonina and Lena drove to Mississippi for Christmas. If it sounds crazy not to fly, rest assured that we had our reasons.

Like many people who tend to get depressed, my dad has never been at his best around the holidays. When I was small, he would often warn me in early November that there would most likely be no presents that year. Around December 1, he would again tell me that we would probably have no money for gifts but would ask me what I might like to get in the event that he could scrape together enough to buy me something small. When Christmas finally rolled around, I would be deluged with presents. As I tore into the packages, he never failed to morosely observe that unlike me, he had been unlucky as a child and never received much more than an orange or an apple and sometimes not even those.

The first few years that my wife and I were together we went to my parents' place for the holidays. Invariably, on

Christmas Eve, my dad picked a fight with one or both of us. One year we argued about Bill Clinton. Another year we argued about Catholicism. After each of these arguments, he would quit speaking to us, and I'd start having flashbacks. If we'd flown to Mississippi, we either had to sit there and suffer until our return flight or pay an exorbitant fine for changing it. After getting burned several times, we quit going. But since our daughters wanted to see their grandparents, we'd decided to risk it again, while leaving ourselves the option of driving away at the first sign of trouble. To make up for the six days they were going to spend on the road, I promised the girls that we would do something special on the way back: detour through Archer City, Texas, and see where *The Last Picture Show* had been filmed. Both of them had read the book and seen the movie, and Antonina had read all the *Lonesome Dove* novels, too, as well as four or five other McMurtry titles. At that point she considered him her favorite writer and still loves his work today, when she's nearly thirty.

Our visit to my parents passed with surprising ease, and we left their house early on the morning of Friday, the twenty-sixth. We drove hard all day, but it was already dark when we turned onto TX-25 North, for the final eleven miles to Archer City.

Having lived in Oxford, Mississippi—for a time, directly across the street from William Faulkner's Rowan Oak—I have watched countless visitors from all over the US and a host of foreign countries react to their first sight of the real world that inspired the fictional world in which they have spent so many fruitful hours. I have seen them weep, and I have seen them display the quiet reverence one might witness in St. Peter's Basilica or the Sistine Chapel. Anyone who doubts the power of a novelist to inflame a reader's imagination might want to spend a few minutes observing literary pilgrims approaching Faulkner's veranda or walking around the Courthouse Square, which, except for the notable presence of a couple hundred automobiles and one-way traffic, looks pretty much as it did when Luster drove Benjy downtown in the surrey in *The Sound and the Fury*. The same Confederate soldier still gazes "with empty eyes beneath his marble hand into wind and weather."

When we pulled into Archer City that night thirteen years ago, the wind was blowing hard, and I could see from the dashboard display that the temperature was in the mid-thirties. As if on cue, right after we passed the Royal Theater and stopped for a red light at the town's main intersection, a tumbleweed bounced across the pavement.

Antonina was sitting beside me. With no small measure of wonder, she said, "This is where the cattle truck from Oklahoma ran over poor Billy."

We parked in front of a diner that I suspected had provided the inspiration for Sam the Lion's all-night café, but the Friday night catfish feast advertised in the window appealed to no one but me. So we proceeded to the Dairy Queen, where we found the walls decorated with cover photos of McMurtry's books, most prominent among them

Walter Benjamin at the Dairy Queen. We spent the night at the Lonesome Dove Inn, instantly recognizable as the former hospital where Sonny recuperated after Duane bashed his eye with a beer bottle. The innkeeper, whose name I no longer recall, told me that she was the sister of the woman who most locals thought was the model for Jacy Farrow, and she sold me an autographed copy of her sister's book, titled—appropriately, I can only suppose, since I never got around to reading it—*Whatever Happened to Jacy Farrow.*

I had an enjoyable conversation with the innkeeper the next morning, while waiting for Ewa and the girls to get dressed. Some years earlier McMurtry had bought a house in town, and he'd also turned several old buildings into a massive book complex called Booked Up. We planned to visit it after breakfast, and I asked the innkeeper if she thought perhaps McMurtry would be there. She said word was, he was not presently in town. "He's got allergies," she told me, "and this is a bad time of year for them, because of all the wind and dust."

I told her I was a novelist and that I knew there were more than a few people in my hometown who did not necessarily relish the publication of my books. I said I'd heard that local people got irate with McMurtry for his portrayal of them in *The Last Picture Show* and I wondered if they were still mad. She said that while McMurtry thought they felt plenty of animosity for him, she did not agree. For one thing, she said, the legacy of the book and movie, along with the book complex itself, brought the town most of its business. "When you walk up and down Main Street," she said, "you'll probably see license plates from several different states, even during the holidays." She shrugged. "If it hadn't been for that book and movie," she said, "you and your family probably wouldn't be here. We're not really on the way to anywhere else."

After breakfast, we visited Booked Up, which if I recall correctly consisted of four different buildings, all of them open and all but one of them unstaffed. Signs near the doors instructed customers to carry any books they wanted to purchase down to the main building and pay for them there. Theft, apparently, was not a concern. While my family lingered in the contemporary fiction annex, wondering how many books they could pile into the Volvo wagon, I spent some time walking the streets. I stopped for a while in front of the Royal Theater, the closure of which signals the passing of an era in *The Last Picture Show*, and I also walked into the diner, fully expecting to see Genevieve Morgan behind the counter, wearing her green waitress uniform. Except for her absence, it looked just like I thought it would.

To say that I was moved would be an understatement. I had stepped into a world that I both had and had not ever set foot in before. This duality remains as mysterious to me now as it was that Saturday. I have only experienced it so intensely on one other occasion: the day a couple of years ago when I entered London's Paddington Hilton to ask for directions and had an uncanny sense that I had been there before, though I was on my first trip to the UK; the eerie feeling troubled me all afternoon, so that evening I looked the Hilton up and discovered that it had once been known as The Great Western Royal Hotel, immortalized in William Trevor's short story "Lovers of Their Time," about a couple who initiate their illicit romance in an unlocked bathroom, where they make love in a tub with "two monstrous brass taps."

Most places we visit are just places. But occasionally a writer lays claim to one, and it can never again be divorced from the uses to which he or she has put it. Oxford, Mississippi, is one of those. So is Archer City, Texas.

To RETURN TO OUR STARTING POINT: WHAT MAKES US fall in love with certain books?

According to the diary that my mother maintained for several years after my birth—it was called, by the way, "The Baby Book"—I learned to read shortly before my fifth birthday. Whether or not this is true, I can't say. Not because I doubt my mother but because I wonder if I had not memorized the handful of books that she read me over and over. She says that the first one I read aloud from beginning to end was *One Hundred and One Dalmatians*. Online, I have found a condensed adaptation of the 1956 Dodie Smith novel. It looks familiar and was published by Tell-All Books to coincide with the release of the Disney film of the same title, which did in fact come out in 1961, when I turned five. So if what my mother alleges is true, I have been reading novels now for fifty-five years. In other words, I've had plenty of time to develop entrenched aesthetic biases—and maybe even enough time to figure out what they are.

If a novelist's language is simply transparent but fluid, I'll be perfectly happy. Richard Yates falls into that category, William Trevor does, and I would say McMurtry does too. Faulkner doesn't, Joyce doesn't, Woolf doesn't, James Salter doesn't, and I don't think Flannery O'Connor does either: there is far more of these artists' personalities on display, line by line, than one detects in the work of the first three writers, and it's one of the many rewards offered by their novels and stories. If, on the other hand, the novelist seems to me to be a maladroit stylist of whatever ilk, I'll have trouble staying with the book. I could make a list of writers that I think fall into this category, some of them widely praised, but what's the point? I've got a friend who hates Prosecco, but it tastes just fine to me.

I have a hard time admiring a novel with a vaguely realized setting. I want place on the page in all its particulars, so that I can see, hear, smell and taste what the characters do. If we're going to be in a nonspecific place, like we nearly always are in Kafka's work, I still want to see the castle that looms over everything, and I still want to know that it's a place where a cockroach craves sour milk and rotten food and that if you hit him with an apple, it will embed itself in his shell and fester.

With respect to narrative technique, I tend to be drawn to a roving third-person, though it flies in the face of the orthodoxy that many American writers of my generation imbibed in the MFA programs most of us attended. I have often wondered why it appeals to me so much, and while writing these pages I have come up with an answer that seems plausible. Though I have neglected to mention it until now, I play bluegrass music on guitar, mandolin and banjo, and when I'm not listening to bluegrass, it's probably because I'm listening to jazz. I'm happiest where the two genres overlap, as they do in the music of David Grisman, Tony Rice, Bela Fleck, Alison Brown, Grant Gordy, Mark O'Connor, and various others. Both jazz and bluegrass, as quite a few critics have pointed out, are democratic: they allow each member of the band a chance to solo, to make his or her own statement on nearly every tune. The multiple third-person, practiced so effortlessly by McMurtry in *The Last Picture Show*, achieves the same affect. Sonny Crawford is without question at the center of the novel, but all the other major characters, as well as quite a few of the minor ones, are given their own perspectives too. We know what the world looks like to them, not just how they and the rest of the world look to Sonny.

And isn't it natural, really, for one to want the world to know how it looks from where he or she is standing? Isn't that, in fact, the reason most of us who write fiction ever began to do it? I reminded myself of this some years ago when I was still teaching at Fresno State, on a day when one of my students explained what he found most appealing about the work of Junot Díaz: "In his stories Díaz is saying 'Here's how it feels to be me,'" my student told the class. "He's saying, 'If you don't like it, I don't fucking give a shit.'" He made this statement after informing us that while he could always "get into" Díaz," Richard Ford's story "Communist" had left him cold because the narrator was someone he just couldn't relate to. I gently argued with him a while, pointing out that whether he could relate to the narrator or not, surely he could appreciate how Ford managed to make all of us think we knew certain things about the character that had never been directly stated—that he'd probably never had a satisfying relationship, that he'd moved around a lot and had never found what most of us would call a home—and how Ford presented such a finely textured landscape in his depiction of rural Montana. My student grudgingly admitted that those were useful skills for a writer to be able to call upon, but it was clear that for him the higher value was the blunt honesty he identified in the work of Díaz.

Did he see himself reflected in Díaz's stories? Unlike so many Díaz characters, he did not come from an economically disadvantaged ethnic background. Instead, he'd grown up in an extremely affluent and nearly all-white community in Southern California. He was, however, mildly autistic, and whereas both of his sisters had attended prestigious private colleges, he'd only gotten accepted at a lower-tier state university. He had a rich and often disturbing imagination. Though he struggled with grammar and syntax, on nearly every page of his own fiction there would be at least one image or one line of dialogue so arresting that I would still be thinking about it a few days later.

Díaz's work spoke to him more insistently than it speaks to me. I don't need to apologize for that. But neither does he.

•

What strikes me at the end of these musings is just how long *The Last Picture Show* has continued to speak to me. The first time I read it, I was the same age as Sonny Crawford. Now I'm probably about as old as Sam the Lion, and my hair is nearly white, just like his. My life has changed enormously since I opened the book that first time. Back then, I'd spent all but a few weeks of it in the same Mississippi Delta county, and I'd never been out of the South. Not to put too fine a point on it, I'd never been laid. I'd never even had a real girlfriend. Since then, I've gotten married, helped raise two great young women, traveled a fair amount, lived in six different states and one foreign country, where my wife and I still own a flat. I've had surgery twice and almost died once. Gangrene.

I have read a lot of novels, too, and I've forgotten most of them. Unless I'm teaching a particular book, I seldom go back and reread. I could fairly easily make a list of the exceptions, the smattering of novels I've read more than once. Until I was about twenty, I frequently returned to *Huckleberry Finn*, though the last few times I didn't reread it from start to finish, just went back over my favorite passages. I'm sorry to say I haven't opened it in at least

twenty-five years, since teaching it in a sophomore literature class at Fresno State. I used to reread *The Sound and
the Fury* every few years, but it's been a decade or so since I
did that. I've read all of Richard Yates's novels twice, and I
hope to make the trip at least once more before I contemplate my final period. I've read a few of Graham Greene's
novels twice and my favorite, *The Human Factor*, four times.
I've read *Beloved*, *Wise Blood*, and *Anna Karenina* twice, the
last of these in two different translations, which effectively
turned it into two different books. I've read all of Kundera
twice and *The Unbearable Lightness of Being* three times.

The list of very good or even great novels that I've never
felt compelled to return to is infinitely more impressive. It
includes *War and Peace, Madame Bovary, Absalom, Absalom!,
Mrs. Dalloway, Crime and Punishment, Pride and Prejudice,
One Hundred Years of Solitude, Ulysses,* Michael Tournier's
The Ogre, William T. Vollman's *Europe Central*, Edward P.
Jones's *The Known World*, and most of the others I've ever
loved or admired. I'm not arguing that this is in any way
laudable, just admitting that I seldom go back.

Yet I've never stayed away from *The Last Picture Show*
for more than a couple of years. If I don't reread the novel, I
watch the film again. Even after all this time, the book and
the movie keep yielding new discoveries. Until my most
recent reading, for instance, I didn't realize that the accident that killed Sonny's mother, which we are told about
in a single line of exposition in chapter three, and the one
that takes Billy's life at the end of the book both involve

cattle trucks. It's as if the author is hinting that if you live in Thalia long enough, sooner or later you may well get run over by an eighteen-wheeler that reeks of manure.

There's a deeper reason, though, that I keep coming back to this tale, and I've known for a long time what it is. When my friend Rev loaned me his father's copy of the novel when I was seventeen years old, he was handing me the book that would convince me that lives like mine, and those of the people I saw around me in a place I hated at least as much as I loved it, were worth an infinite number of stories. All I needed to do was live a little more and listen a whole lot.

Though McMurtry has always denied that Thalia is Archer City, or that his novel was based on anything real, he included the following note up front: "*The Last Picture Show* is lovingly dedicated to my home town." The pages you've just read are lovingly dedicated to mine.

The *Bookmarked* Series

CPSIA information can be obtained
at www.ICGtesting.com
Printed in the USA
LVOW03s2258080817
544314LV00003B/3/P